Leaders of the Americas

North America

South America

Leaders of the Americas

Short Biographies and Dialogs

Book 1

William P. Pickett

Passaic High School

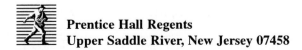

Prentice Hall Regents
Upper Saddle River, New Jersey 07458

Library of Congress Cataloging-in-Publication Data

Pickett, William P.
    Leaders of the Americas / William P. Pickett.
        p.   cm.
    Includes bibliographical references.
    Contents: bk.   1. Short biographies and dialogs.
    ISBN 0-13-102484-1
    1. Readers—Biography.   2. English language—Textbooks for foreign
speakers.   3. United States—Biography—Problems, exercises, etc.
4. Latin America—Biography—Problems, exercises, etc.   I. Title.
PE1127.B53P53   1995
428.6´4—dc20
                                                                94-9558
                                                                    CIP
                                                                     AC

Acquisitions Editor: Nancy Baxer
Project Management: J. Carey Publishing Service
Interior Design: Noel Vreeland Carter
Cover Design: Marianne Frasco
Illustrations: Theresa Troise Heidel
Buyer: Raymond Keating

©1995 by Prentice Hall Regents
Prentice-Hall, Inc.
A Simon & Schuster Company
Upper Saddle River, New Jersey 07458

Printed in the United States of America

10   9   8   7   6   5   4

ISBN 0-13-102484-1

Prentice-Hall International (UK) Limited, *London*
Prentice-Hall of Australia Pty. Limited, *Sydney*
Prentice-Hall Canada Inc., *Toronto*
Prentice-Hall Hispanoamericana, S.A., *Mexico*
Prentice-Hall of India Private Limited, *New Delhi*
Prentice-Hall of Japan, Inc., *Tokyo*
Prentice-Hall of Southeast Asia Pte. Ltd., *Singapore*
Editora Prentice-Hall do Brasil, Ltda., *Rio de Janeiro*

Photograph and illustration credits begin on page 203.

In Memory of My Brother Edward

Contents

Preface

Overview

Leaders of the Americas is a reader that introduces students to some of the most influential people in the history of North and South America. It is divided into two books. Book 1 starts with Christopher Columbus sailing to America and ends with Orville Wright's historic flight at Kitty Hawk.

The heart of each of its 21 chapters is a short biography of an American leader and two dialogs highlighting an event or two in the leader's life.

Book 2 will feature biographies and dialogs of more recent American leaders.

Level

Leaders of the Americas is written for advanced beginners or low intermediates. The book presupposes that its readers know the most common English structures and words. At the same time, structures and vocabulary are controlled to keep the book at a level appropriate for advanced beginners or low intermediates.

Objectives

Leaders of the Americas aims to:

1. Increase reading skills
2. Increase students' knowledge of and interest in famous American leaders
3. Expand vocabulary
4. Increase speaking skills through discussion and dialogs

Leaders may also be used to improve writing. In this case, students would write out their answers to the comprehension questions and write about some of the topics in the discussion sections. Students can also use the biographies in *Leaders* as models for biographies they write.

Leaders aims to be interesting, enjoyable, and informative. Students learn to read by reading, and if the students enjoy reading this book, they will learn a lot from it.

Contents

Every biography in *Leaders* begins with a picture or drawing of the leader, or some important event in the leader's life, or a map. The students' prior knowledge of the leaders is usually slight, so they need this visual help. Each chapter also begins with a list of the important events in the life of the leader.

Two preview statements follow. The purpose of the preview statements is to give the students some background information, to arouse their interest, and, in some cases, to relate the biography to today's world.

The biography follows. However, the chapters about Columbus, the Pilgrims, and Lewis and Clark are not so much biographies as histories of important events.

Following the biography, there are comprehension questions, some of which ask the students to go beyond the text to infer, judge, and guess. This type of question also occurs in the discussion questions.

After the comprehension questions, the more difficult words in the biography are listed. These are called key words. These words are placed after the story, since it is hoped that the context of the story will shed some light on their meaning, and that the teacher will not have to spend too much time on them.

However, vocabulary development is an important aim of *Leaders*, and a cloze exercise follows. The cloze paragraphs summarize the biography and test and reinforce the vocabulary used in it.

Two dialogs follow. They are about an interesting event or two in the life of the leader. While the biographies are factual, the dialogs are obviously a combination of imagination and facts. They are generally based on an historical occurrence, but the dialog itself, of course, is created by the author. All of the characters in the dialogs are real except the "reporters," Margarita on pages 8 and 9, Ann on pages 36 and 37, and the colonel on pages 142 and 143.

Five words are left out of each dialog and must be filled in by the students. This makes the students more active. Students also enjoy and benefit from roleplaying the dialogs.

After the dialogs, there is a discussion section in which the students make their own comments and express their own ideas, feelings, and reactions. These discussions can take place in small groups or with the entire class.

Sections of the Declaration of Independence and the Constitution of the United States, and the entire Gettysburg Address are included as supplements to Chapters 4, 5, and 10. An introduction and vocabulary notes are provided to help students understand these documents.

To encourage students to do extensive reading, each chapter closes with a list of books that are easy to read. These books are classified as level 1, 2, or 3. Level 1 books are the easiest available, but they are generally more difficult than the readings in *Leaders*. Still, most students should be able to read them. Level 2 books will be difficult for most students and impossible for some. Level 3 books have an asterisk and are for teachers. They are too difficult for advanced beginners or low intermediates. Many of the books listed are available in the children's sections of public libraries.

A Word List, Review Tests, and an Answer Key

A word list has been placed in the back of the book. Review tests for each unit, and an answer key have been put in a separate booklet. The tests consist of vocabulary and true/false questions.

Audience

Leaders is written for young adults and adults of all ages. It is aimed at junior high school, high school, community college, and adult education students, as well as at college programs that accept beginning ESL students. It is written for ESL students living in North and South America and should also appeal to students in other countries, to the extent that they are interested in reading about American leaders.

Content-based ESL

Leaders is a content-based reader and should appeal to those who favor content-based ESL instruction. And while *Leaders* is not a history book, its readers will learn a lot of history, and the book will prepare them for their history courses.

Relationship to The Pizza Tastes Great and The Chicken Smells Good

The biographies and dialogs of *Leaders of the Americas* are very different from the stories and the dialogs of two other books by the same author, *The Pizza Tastes Great* and *The Chicken Smells Good*. *The Pizza* and *The Chicken* feature ordinary people and everyday happenings. *Leaders* is about extraordinary people and events that have changed the Americas. Hopefully, students will enjoy reading about the great leaders of the

Americas as much as they have enjoyed reading about the ordinary people of *The Pizza* and *The Chicken*.

Like *The Pizza* and *The Chicken*, *Leaders of the Americas* is a combination of brief stories and dialogs. Like them, it leads to discussion, and its principal aim is to be interesting. The style of *Leaders* is also similar to that of *The Pizza* and *The Chicken*, and those who like *The Pizza* and *The Chicken* will probably like *Leaders*. *Leaders*, however, is a lot more difficult than *The Pizza* and somewhat more difficult than *The Chicken*.

Acknowledgments

I wish to thank Nancy Baxer, Nancy Leonhardt, Anne Riddick, Dominick Mosco, and Jack Ross of Prentice Hall Regents for their help and encouragement in writing *Leaders of the Americas*. I am also grateful to Jennifer Carey, the project manager, for her able assistance.

I thank Barbara Buono of Passaic High School for helping to field test *Leaders*, and Gale Motaski, Rose Sanz, Marvin Walker, and Margaret Darragh, also of Passaic High School, for reviewing parts of the text.

Above all, I am grateful to my wife, Dorothy, for her careful review of *Leaders* and her many helpful suggestions.

Leaders of the Americas

1

Early Leaders

1 Christopher Columbus

The Santa Maria

Important Events

1451	Columbus is born in Genoa, Italy
August 3, 1492	Sails from Spain for the Indies
October 12, 1492	Lands on an island off the coast of America
March 15, 1493	Arrives back in Spain and receives many honors
1493, 1498, 1502	Makes second, third, and fourth voyages to America
May 20, 1506	Dies in Spain

Preview

1. Columbus landed in America in 1492, and many history books say that he discovered America. But did he? The Native Americans he called Indians were in America long before Columbus. Leif Erickson, a sailor from Norway, came to America in 1,000 A.D.

2. Imagine trying to cross the Atlantic Ocean in a small ship without a motor, without contact with land, without knowing how far you had to go. This is what Columbus and his sailors did.

Columbus Sails to America

Christopher Columbus was an Italian sea captain with a dream that he hoped would lead to fame and riches. He dreamed of sailing to the Indies[1] and returning with the gold and spices of the East. He thought that the world was round, so he planned to sail west from Europe and to cross the Atlantic Ocean. He thought that it was only 2,400 miles to the Indies. Most Europeans agreed that the world was round, but they said it was 10,000 miles to the Indies, much too far to sail. Columbus, however, wasn't afraid to try the impossible.

But he needed money for his trip. He needed it to pay the sailors, to buy supplies, and to pay for the ships he planned to use. He went to the King of Portugal, but the king wouldn't help. Then he went to Queen Isabella of Spain. It took her six years to decide, but she finally gave him the money. She thought Columbus was brave and had a good idea.

On August 3, 1492, Columbus and three ships, the Niña, the Pinta, and the Santa María sailed west from Spain and started their voyage across the Atlantic Ocean. Columbus was on the Santa María, the largest of the three ships. Columbus and his sailors didn't know that America existed.

Helped by good weather and strong winds, the ships sailed for many days, but the sailors didn't see land. They were tired and afraid they wouldn't be able to get back to Spain. They weren't happy with Columbus and wanted to return, but he persuaded them to continue. He promised to turn back if they didn't see land in three days.

It was two AM, the morning of October 12, 1492. In the moonlight, one of the sailors saw land. It was an island; it was America! But the sailors and Columbus didn't know this. They thought that they were close to Japan and that the people on the island were from the Indies. So they called them Indians.

Columbus named the island San Salvador. There was no gold and there were no cities on San Salvador, but Columbus and his sailors were happy to be on land. The Native Americans they met were friendly, and Columbus made six of the natives go with them. Then he sailed west to

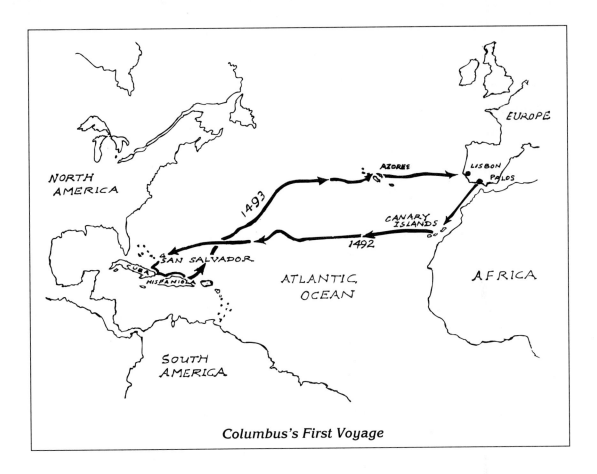

Columbus's First Voyage

Cuba and east to the island of Hispaniola[2] before returning to Spain. He arrived in Spain on March 15, 1493 and received many honors.

1 The **Indies** included India, Japan, and China.
2 **Hispaniola** is a large island 90 miles east of Cuba. Today the western part of the island is Haiti, and the eastern part is the Dominican Republic.

I. Comprehension

Answer these questions about the story. Use your own ideas to answer the questions marked with a check ✔.

Paragraph 1

1. Where did Columbus want to go? Why?
2. What made him think he could go to the Indies by sailing west?

Paragraph 2

    3. Why did he need money for the trip?

    4. What did Queen Isabella think of him? And of his trip?

Paragraph 3

    5. Name the three ships Columbus took. On which ship did he sail?

Paragraph 4

    6. What did the sailors fear?

✔ 7. Columbus's sailors wanted to return to Spain, but he persuaded them to continue. What does that tell us about him?

Paragraph 5

    8. What did one of the sailors see?

    9. What did Columbus and his sailors call the people on the island? Why?

Paragraph 6

    10. What word is used to describe the Native Americans?

✔ 11. Why do you think Columbus took some Native Americans back to Spain?

    12. Where did he go after he left San Salvador?

II. Key Words

Before studying these words, reread the story and try to guess their meaning.

Nouns		Verbs	Irregular Pasts	Adjectives
captain	sailors	sail (+n.)	thought - think	round
dream (+v.)	supplies	agree	said - say	brave
fame	ship (+v.)	decide	went - go	native (+n.)
gold	voyage	get back	took - take	
spice	wind	return (+n.)	gave - give	**Other**
East (+adv., adj.)	moonlight	turn back	saw - see	west (adv., n., adj.)
		persuade	met - meet	finally (adv.)
			made - make	

III. Story Completion

Complete the story with these words.

brave	persuaded	dream	finally	agreed
moonlight	spices	turn back	far	supplies

Trying the Impossible

Columbus's _____ was to become rich and famous by sailing to the Indies and bringing back gold and _____ from the East.

He thought the world was round and many in Europe _____, but they said it was too _____ to sail to the Indies. Columbus, however, was _____ and wanted to try what seemed impossible.

Columbus needed money to pay for the ships and the sailors, and to buy _____. The King of Portugal wouldn't help, and it took Queen Isabella six years to decide, but she _____ said yes.

The Niña, the Pinta, and the Santa María sailed for days, but the sailors didn't see land. They were afraid and wanted to _____. But Columbus _____ them to continue.

In the _____, one of the sailors saw an island. It was America, but Columbus and his sailors didn't know it. They were very happy to see land.

IV. Dialogs

Key Words

Nouns	Verbs	Adjectives
appointment	be born	crazy
luck	cross (+n.)	expensive

A Special Voyage

Columbus wants to see the queen of Spain to ask her for money for his trip to the Indies. He's talking to Margarita, the queen's secretary.

Complete the dialog with these words.

queen   born   expensive   appointment   captain

Margarita: What's your name?

Columbus: Christopher Columbus. I'm a sea _____.

Margarita: Where are you from?

Columbus: Italy. I was _____ in Genoa.

Margarita: And how can I help you?

Columbus: I want an _____ to see the _____.

Margarita: Why?

Columbus: I need money for a special voyage.

Margarita: Where do you plan to go?

Columbus: To the Indies.

Margarita: Mm. That is special!

Columbus: Yes, and very _____.

I'm Going to Sail West

Columbus and the queen's secretary are discussing his plan to go to the Indies.

Complete the dialog with these words.

crazy   **luck**   **cross**   **round**   **ship**

Margarita: How are you going to the Indies?

Columbus: By _____. I'm going to sail west.

Margarita: And _____ the Atlantic Ocean?

Columbus: That's right.

Margarita: Are you _____? That's impossible.

Columbus: No it isn't. The world is _____.

Margarita: I know, but it's much too far to the Indies. It's 10,000 miles.

Columbus: I don't think so. I have to try.

Margarita: Okay. You can see the queen tomorrow afternoon. Good

_____!

Columbus: Thanks. I'll need it.

V. Sharing Ideas

Discuss these questions in pairs or small groups.

1. Why is it easier and safer to cross the Atlantic in a ship today than in 1492?
2. What were some of the supplies that Columbus and his sailors needed for their voyage?
3. Columbus didn't discover America, but he discovered some things about America, things that Europeans didn't know. What did he discover about America?
4. Columbus called the people he saw in America "Indians." But today most think it's better and clearer to call them Native Americans. What do you think? Explain your answer.

5. In what way was the coming of Columbus and the Europeans bad for Native Americans?

6. Some say that Columbus was a hero, but others say no. They say he started a sad history of abuse in which thousands of Native Americans lost their lands, their cultures, and their lives. Is Columbus a hero or not? What do you think?

7. What countries do you think celebrate the coming of Columbus to America?

8. What places and things can you think of that are named after Columbus?

VI. Books You May Enjoy

1. de Kaye, James T. *Meet Christopher Columbus.* Set-up Paperback Books. New York: Random House, 1989. 72 pp. (Level 1)

2. Stein, R. Conrad. *The Story of Christopher Columbus.* Cornerstones of Freedom. Chicago: Childrens Press, 1992. 32 pp. (Level 2)

3. Fritz, Jean *Where Do You Think You're Going, Christopher Columbus?* New York: G.P. Putnam's Sons, 1980. 80 pp. (Level 2)

4. Osborne, Mary Pope. *The Story of Christopher Columbus, Admiral of the Ocean Sea.* Dell Yearling Biography. New York: Dell Publishing, 1987. 90 pp. (Level 2)

2 The Pilgrims

The First Thanksgiving

Important Events

September 16, 1620	The Pilgrims sail from England in the Mayflower
November 21, 1620	Arrive at Cape Cod, Massachusetts
November 21, 1620	Sign the Mayflower Compact
December 21, 1620	Land at Plymouth, Massachusetts
March 22, 1621	Sign peace treaty with Massasoit
Fall, 1621	Celebrate first Thanksgiving

Preview

1. To come to America from England in 1620 was difficult. The trip was long — 76 days. The food was poor. There were no beds on the ship for the passengers. Compare this to how most immigrants come to the United States today.

2. To come to America, the Pilgrims had to leave relatives, friends, and a country they loved. And they had to learn to live in a very different country. Is this also true of the immigrants of today? Explain your answer.

The Pilgrims

On September 16, 1620, 102 passengers sailed from England to North America on the Mayflower. Many of the passengers were going to America so they could worship God freely. They didn't want to go to the king's church, the Church of England. They wanted to have a separate church, and that's why they were called Separatists. Another name for them was the Pilgrims.

The Mayflower ran into some bad storms and sailed for 76 days before it finally arrived at Cape Cod, Massachusetts on November 21, 1620. The Pilgrims were far to the north of the Virginia Colony where they planned to settle. The men on the Mayflower met and decided to stay where they were and to govern themselves. They signed an agreement to make their own laws and to obey them. This agreement was called the Mayflower Compact. It was the beginning of self-government in America.

Some of the Pilgrims explored the area looking for a place where they could settle permanently. On December 21, 1620, they found one with a small stream and a field where they could grow corn. It was Plymouth, Massachusetts, not far from Cape Cod. Their first winter there was terrible. It was cold, and their food was poor. Many of them became sick, and half of them died. But they had great courage. When the Mayflower returned to England, all of them chose to stay in Plymouth.

In the spring, two friendly Native Americans, Samoset and Squanto, came to the Pilgrims' aid. Both spoke English and taught them many things about the area and the local Native Americans. Squanto showed them how to plant corn and to fish. They also brought Massasoit, a Native American chief, to meet John Carver, the Governor of Plymouth. Massasoit was friendly, and after he had a long talk with the Governor, they signed a peace treaty. This was the beginning of many years of peace between the Pilgrims and Massasoit's tribe.

After a good harvest in the fall of 1621, the Pilgrims had plenty of food. They were happy and grateful. They invited their Native American friends to a three-day celebration to thank God and their friends. There

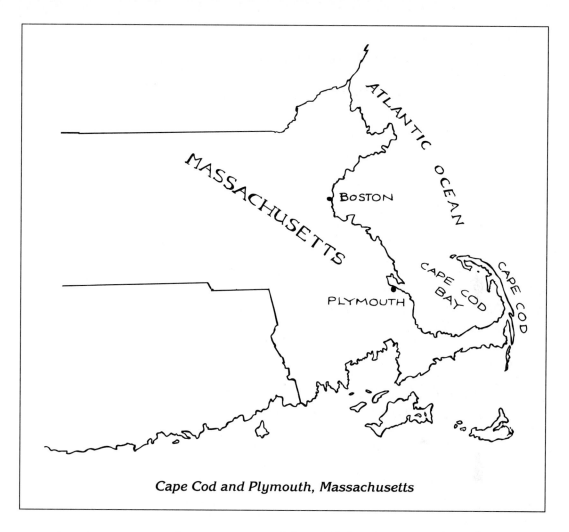

Cape Cod and Plymouth, Massachusetts

were prayers, a parade, games, and lots of food, including turkey, fish, deer meat, corn, and pumpkin. This was the first celebration of Thanksgiving.

I. Comprehension

Answer these questions about the story. Use your own ideas to answer questions marked with a check ✔.

Paragraph 1

1. What was the name of the ship that sailed to North America? How many passengers were on it?
2. Why were many of the passengers going to America?

Paragraph 2

✔ 3. Why was it that only the men on the Mayflower met to decide what to do?

4. What was the name of their agreement?

5. Why was it so important?

Paragraph 3

6. What happened to the Pilgrims during their first winter in Plymouth?

7. How many of them returned to England?

Paragraph 4

8. What did Squanto show the Pilgrims?

✔ 9. Why was it important that the Pilgrims learn how to fish?

10. Who signed the peace treaty?

Paragraph 5

11. Why did the Pilgrims have a three-day celebration?

12. How did the Pilgrims and their Native American friends celebrate?

II. Key Words

Before studying these words, reread the story and try to guess their meaning.

Nouns		Verbs	Irregular Pasts	Adjectives
passenger	chief	worship (+n.)	ran (into) - run	separate (+v.)
church	governor	settle	found - find	terrible
storm	treaty	govern	became - become	local
agreement	tribe	sign (+n.)	chose - choose	plenty (of)
compact	harvest (+v.)	obey	came - come	grateful
self-government	celebration	explore	brought - bring	
stream (+v.)	turkey	show how		**Other**
courage	deer	plant (+n.)		permanently
aid (+v.)	pumpkin	include		(adv.)

III. Story Completion

Complete the story with these words.

courage	separate	harvest	signed	chief
stream	agreement	chose	storms	settle

Going to America

The Pilgrims didn't want to go to the Church of England. They wanted a _____ church. So they left England on the Mayflower and sailed for America in September 1620.

They ran into some bad _____ crossing the Atlantic Ocean and arrived at Cape Cod, far north of where they wanted to be. The men on the Mayflower met and made a (an) _____ called the Mayflower Compact, which they all _____.

The Pilgrims landed at Cape Cod and looked for a place to _____. They discovered one with a _____ and a field where they could grow corn. It was called Plymouth. Their first winter there was terrible, but when the Mayflower returned to England, all of the Pilgrims _____ to stay in America. They were men and women of great _____.

Massasoit, a Native American _____, and John Carver, the Governor of Plymouth, made a peace treaty. And in the fall of 1621, the Pilgrims had a good _____ and plenty of food. So they invited their

Native American friends to a three-day celebration, the first
Thanksgiving.

IV. Dialogs

Key Words

Nouns		Verbs		Adjective	Other
protection	hire	miss (+n.)		lonely	either (adv., adj., pron., conj.)
defense	train	suggest			
friendship	I'd = I would	shall			

The Pilgrims Need a Soldier

Miles Standish isn't a Pilgrim, but he is a soldier, and the Pilgrims want
him to go with them on the Mayflower. He is talking about this with his
wife, Rose.

Complete the dialog with these words.

protection   **miss**   **train**   **lonely**   **hire**

Miles: I have some important news.

Rose: What is it?

Miles: I'm going to America on the Mayflower.

Rose: Are you serious?

Miles: Very. The Pilgrims want to _____ me.

Rose: Why?

Miles: They need a soldier.

Rose: What for?

Miles: For _____. The Indians or French may attack them.

Rose: But what good is one soldier?

Miles: I'll _____ others.

Rose: Now I understand. I want to go with you.

Miles: And I want you to come. I'd be very _____ without you.

Rose: And I'd _____ you so much.

A Peace Treaty

The Wampanoags are a Native American tribe. In March 1621, Massasoit, their chief, and Governor Carver meet and make a peace treaty. Squanto acts as an interpreter.

Complete the dialog with these words.

friendship   suggest   treaty   either   defense

Massasoit: I'm the chief of the Wampanoags.

Carver: And I'm the Governor of Plymouth. Welcome!

Massasoit: Thank you.

Carver: Would you like a drink?

Massasoit: Sure. This is good.

Carver: I'm glad you like it.

Massasoit: The Wampanoags want to be your friends.

Carver: I was hoping they would.

Massasoit: Why don't we make a peace _____?

Carver: Good idea. What do you _____? What shall we say?

Massasoit: The Wamponoags will never carry arms when we're with the Pilgrims.

Carver: And when we're with the Wamponoags, we won't

_____.

Massasoit: If anyone attacks the Pilgrims, we'll come to your

_____.

Carver: And we'll do same if you're attacked.

Massasoit: This treaty will bring peace.

Carver: And _____. I'll sign for the Pilgrims.

Massasoit: And I'll sign for the Wampanoags.

V. Sharing Ideas

Discuss these questions in pairs or small groups.

1. The Pilgrims came to America to be free. Do people still come to the United States to be free? Give an example.
2. Today, why do most immigrants come to the United States?
3. If you're from another country, why did you come?
4. Cold weather was a problem for the Pilgrims when they arrived in Plymouth. Was it a problem for you when you came to the United States? Is it still a problem?
5. The Pilgrims thanked God and the Native Americans for their help. Complete this sentence. I'm grateful to _____.
6. Name some things for which you're grateful.
7. Do you like turkey? Do you have turkey for Thanksgiving?
8. Every Thanksgiving a group of Wampanoags meet at Plymouth not to celebrate, but for a day of mourning or sorrow. Why?

VI. Books You May Enjoy

1. Richards, Norman. *The Story of the Mayflower Compact.* Cornerstones of Freedom. Chicago: Childrens Press, 1967. 31 pp. (Level 2)

2. Seawall, Marcia. *The Pilgrims of Plymouth.* New York: Macmillan Publishing Company, 1986. 48 pp. (Level 2)

3. Groh, Lynn. *The Pilgrims: Brave Settlers of Plymouth.* Champaign, Illinois: Garrard Publishing Company, 1968. (Level 2)

4. Beck, Barbara L. *The Pilgrims of Plymouth.* A First Book. New York: Franklin Watts, Inc., 1972. 89 pp. (Level 2)

3 Samuel de Champlain

Samuel de Champlain

	Important Events
1570 (?)	Champlain is born in Brouage, France
March 15, 1603	Makes first voyage to Canada
July 3, 1608	Founds Quebec
July 1609	Discovers Lake Champlain: battle with Iroquois
1613	Publishes *Les Voyages*
March 23, 1633	Makes last voyage to Canada
December 25, 1635	Dies in Quebec

Preview

1. Samuel de Champlain was a great French explorer who devoted his life to exploring and settling New France (Canada). He founded the city of Quebec in 1608. Today most of the people in the province of Quebec are French Canadians and speak French. Montreal is the second largest French-speaking city in the world.

2. Canada is a land of lakes and rivers. And Champlain spent much time exploring the St. Lawrence River, Lake Ontario, and Lake Huron. He also explored the coast of Canada and New England and crossed the Atlantic 29 times. But he never learned to swim!

Samuel de Champlain, Father of New France
(1570? – 1635)

Samuel de Champlain was born in Brouage, France, around 1570. His father was a sailor and that's what Samuel always wanted to be. Although he never learned to swim, Champlain couldn't wait to go to sea. He also loved to draw and to read about his hero, Jacques Cartier, the great French explorer.

In March 1603, Champlain sailed from France on his first voyage to Canada (New France). He explored the St. Lawrence River, traveling inland past the sites of Quebec and Montreal where Cartier had camped many years ago. Champlain returned to France in September 1603. He went back to Canada in April 1604 and spent the next three years exploring and making maps of the coast of Canada and New England.

In 1608, on his third trip to Canada, Champlain founded Quebec, Canada's oldest city. It soon became the center of fur trading. The settlers bought furs from the Native Americans and shipped them to France. It was a very profitable business.

Champlain loved and respected the Native Americans of New France, and they loved and trusted him because he always tried to treat them fairly. They helped him explore their lands, and he frequently lived and ate with them. But there was a big problem. Champlain's Native American friends and the Iroquois, who lived in New York, were bitter enemies. Champlain led his Native American friends in an attack on an Iroquois tribe. From that day on, the French and the Iroquois were enemies. The battle with the Iroquois took place on the shore of Lake Champlain, a large lake that Champlain had discovered and that he named after himself.

Champlain loved New France and its many rivers, lakes, and forests, and he explored not only the St. Lawrence, but also the Ottawa River, Lake Huron, and Lake Ontario. He knew New France better than any other European, and his dream was to make it a great French colony. He

Samuel de Champlain Exploring New France

wanted people to go there to settle, not just to fish and trade for fur. When he had the opportunity, Champlain went back to France to ask the king to send more settlers and money, but the French court didn't understand how important New France was and never gave him the support he asked for and deserved.

Champlain was also a writer. He wrote books about New France and the Native Americans who lived there. He wrote because he wanted everyone to know about the beauty, riches, and natives of New France, and he wanted people from France to settle there.

Champlain spent the last few years of his life improving Quebec. It was only a small settlement of about 200, but Champlain hoped it would some day be a great French city. Champlain died in Quebec on Christmas Day, 1635, and was buried there. He had devoted 32 years of his life to New France. He was a great leader, explorer, sailor, mapmaker, and writer and is rightly called the Father of New France.

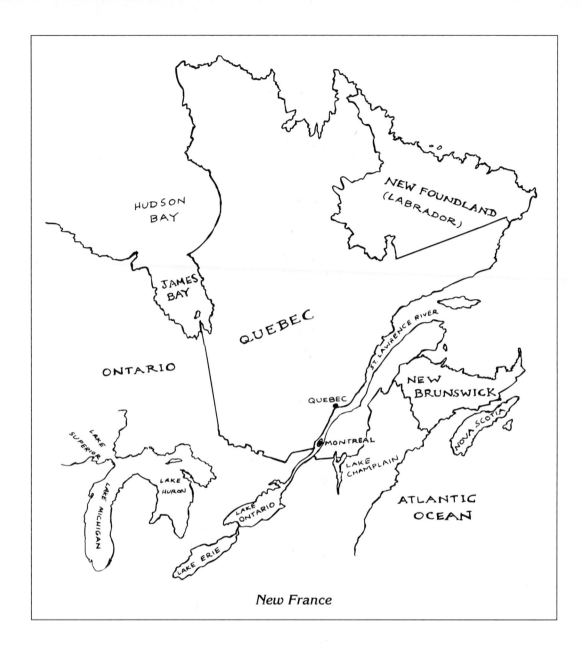

New France

I. Comprehension

Answer these questions about the story. Use your own ideas to answer the questions marked with a check ✔.

Paragraph 1

1. Name two things Champlain loved to do.

Paragraph 2

2. What did Champlain do on his first voyage to Canada?
3. What did he do on his second voyage?

Paragraph 3

4. What was Quebec the center of?

Paragraph 4

5. Why did the Native Americans of New France love and trust Champlain?
✔ 6. How do you think the Native Americans helped him explore?
✔ 7. Do you think Champlain made a mistake in leading an attack on the Iroquois? Explain your answer.

Paragraph 5

8. What was Champlain's dream?
9. What did he want the king to do?

Paragraph 6

10. Why did Champlain write? Give two reasons.

Paragraph 7

11. How did Champlain spend the last few years of his life?
12. Where and when did he die?

II. Key Words

Before studying these words, reread the story and try to guess their meaning.

Nouns		Verbs	Irregular Pasts	Adjective
explorer	shore	draw	spent - spend	profitable
site	forest	found	bought - buy	bitter
settler	colony	respect (+n.)	ate - eat	
settlement	opportunity	treat (+n.)	led - lead	**Other**
fur	support (+v.)	trade (+n.)	knew - know	around
trading	mapmaker	deserve	wrote - write	(prep., adv.)
		improve		although (conj.)
		bury		inland (adv.)
		devote		fairly (adv.)
				took place (idiom)

III. Story Completion

Complete the story with these words.

founded	although	improving	fairly	draw
forests	spent	profitable	trade	led

He Loved New France

Samuel de Champlain was born in Brouage, France. _____ he never learned to swim, he couldn't wait to go to sea. He also loved to _____ and read about his hero Jacques Cartier.

On his first voyage to Canada, Champlain explored the St. Lawrence River. On his second, he _____ three years exploring and making maps of the coast of Canada and New England.

In 1608, Champlain _____ the city of Quebec, which became the center of fur trading, a very _____ business.

Champlain always tried to treat the Native Americans of New France _____. However, he also _____ an attack on the Iroquois. From that day on, the French and the Iroquois were enemies.

Champlain loved New France and its many rivers, lakes, and _____. He wanted people to go there to settle, not just to fish and _____ for fur.

Champlain spent the last few years of his life _____ Quebec. He died in Quebec on Christmas Day, 1635, and was buried there.

IV. Dialogs

Key Words

Nouns		Verbs		Adjective
record (+v.)	priest	find (+n.)	convert (+n.)	funny
passage	combination	protect		

Fish, Furs, and a Northwest Passage

In 1603, Samuel de Champlain made his first trip to New France. François Pont-Grave was the owner and captain of the ship on which he sailed. Pont-Grave and Champlain are talking.

Complete the dialog with these words.

camp	find	sail	look for	records

Pont-Grave: I hear the king wants you to _____ to New France with us.

Champlain: Yes. He wants me to make maps and _____ of the voyage.

Pont-Grave: Good. Do you know what we plan to do?

Champlain: I know you're going to explore the St. Lawrence River.

Pont-Grave: Yes, and we're going to stop at Quebec and Montreal.

Champlain: Didn't Cartier _____ in those places in 1535?

Pont-Grave: Yes, he did.

Champlain: That's wonderful! Cartier is my hero.

Pont-Grave: We're also going to _____ a Northwest Passage to China.

Champlain: Great! If we _____ it, we'll be famous!

Pont-Grave: And very rich!

Champlain: How are we going to pay for our trip?

Pont-Grave: We're going to bring back fish and furs.

Farmers, Soldiers, and Priests

Champlain is talking to King Henri IV of France. Champlain wants the king to send farmers, soldiers, and priests to New France.

Complete the dialog with these words.

understand   **colony**   **convert**   **combination**   **protect**

Henri IV: What does the _____ in New France need?

Champlain: Farmers, soldiers, and priests.

Henri IV: That's a funny _____.

Champlain: Farmers are important because we need more food, especially in the winter.

Henri IV: I _____ that, but why do you need soldiers?

Champlain: To _____ the colony from the British and the Native Americans.

Henri IV: Aren't the Native Americans our friends?

Champlain: The Algonquins and the Hurons are, but not the Iroquois.

Henri IV: And why priests?

Champlain: For the colonists, but especially for the Native Americans.

Henri IV: But they're not Christians.

Champlain: No, they're not, but we hope to _____ them.

V. Sharing Ideas

Discuss these questions in pairs or small groups.

1. Like Champlain, many people like boats and like to ride in them. Do you?
2. Do you like to draw? Are you good at drawing?
3. Do you like to fish? Do you fish much?
4. Do you think it's okay to kill animals to make fur coats? Or are you opposed to this? Explain your answer.
5. Cartier was Champlain's hero. Do you have a hero? If so, who is your hero?
6. Why did Champlain do most of his exploring in Canada by boat?
7. What do you think were some of the dangers and difficulties Champlain faced in exploring Canada?
8. What do you know about Canada? Where is it located? What are its main cities? What is its capital? How large is it? What is its population? Describe its climate. Describe its economy. What kind of government does it have? Have the students work in small groups. Each group should give a brief report answering two or three of the questions. One group should include a map of Canada.

VI. Books You May Enjoy

1. Jacobs, William Jay. *Champlain: A Life of Courage.* Chicago: Franklin Watts, 1994. First Books. 64 pp. (Level 1)

2. Grant, Matthew G. *Champlain: Explorer of New France.* Gallery of Great Americans Series. Mankato, Minnesota: Creative Education, 1974. 30 pp. (Level 1)

3. Edwards, Cecile P. *Champlain: Father of New France.* New York: Abbingdon Press, 1955. 128 pp. (Level 2)

*4. Morison, Samuel Eliot. *Samuel de Champlain: Father of New France.* Boston: Little, Brown & Company, 1972. 299 pp. (Level 3)

* Books with an asterisk are for teachers. They are too difficult for students using *Leaders of the Americas.*

2

Leaders of a
New Country

4 Benjamin Franklin

Benjamin Franklin and his Son Experimenting with a Kite

Important Events

January 17, 1706	Franklin is born in Boston, Massachusetts
September 1723	Runs away to Philadelphia
1728	Opens print shop in Philadelphia with a friend
September 1, 1730	Marries Deborah Reed
December 1732	Publishes *Poor Richard's Almanack*
April 1757	Goes to England to represent Pennsylvania
October 1776	Goes to France as U.S. Minister
April 17, 1790	Dies in Philadelphia at the age of 84

Preview

1. Benjamin Franklin started out in life with no money and only two years of formal education. But he worked hard, had a lot of good ideas, and made friends easily. What do you think of the Franklin formula for success? Hard work + good ideas + good friends = success.

2. Franklin did a lot to improve his community. He started a hospital, a library, a university, and the fire department in Philadelphia. Can you think of some small way in which you can improve your community or school?

Benjamin Franklin
(1706 – 1790)

Benjamin Franklin was born in Boston, Massachusetts on January 17, 1706. He was the fifteenth of 17 children. He went to school for only two years because he had to help his father make candles, but he loved to read and study. Life and books were his teachers. He also loved the sea, was a great swimmer, and wanted to be a sailor, but his father wouldn't let him.

His older brother James was a printer and newspaper publisher, and Ben worked for him as an apprentice for several years. Ben and his brother didn't get along and James even hit him. That's why, at the age of 17, Ben ran away to Philadelphia, where he got a job working with a printer. In 1728, he opened a print shop with a friend. He soon published his own newspaper and, in 1732, an almanac[1] that was a great success. He was a good businessman, worked long hours, and made a lot of money.

Franklin made his money as a printer, writer, and publisher, but he was also a scientist and inventor. He loved to experiment, especially with electricity. By flying a kite in a lightning storm, he proved that lightning was electricity. He also invented a special stove (the Franklin Stove) to heat houses, lightning rods to protect houses, and bifocals.[2] He let everyone use his inventions and never accepted a penny for them.

Franklin was always looking for ways to improve Philadelphia. He helped organize the first hospital and the first fire department in the city, and he started the first lending library in America. He got the city to pave, clean, and improve the lighting of the city streets. He reorganized and improved the postal service.

In 1757, Franklin went to London and spent 16 years there representing Pennsylvania and other colonies. He tried to help the colonies and England maintain good relations, but it became impossible. In 1775, he returned to America, helped write the Declaration of Independence,[3] and signed it.

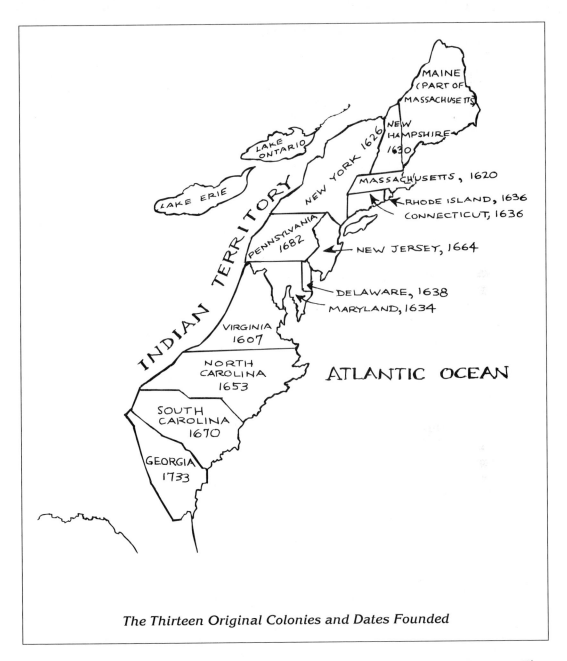

The Thirteen Original Colonies and Dates Founded

In 1777, Franklin became the United States' Minister to France. The war against England wasn't going well, but he used his popularity in France to persuade the French king and other French officials to send money, guns, and soldiers to America. With French help, the United States won the war, and Franklin was able to do what he really wanted to do, arrange peace with England. As he said, "In my opinion there never was a good war or a bad peace." Franklin died in Philadelphia on April 17, 1790, at the age of 84.

1 An **almanac** (spelled almanack in Franklin's time) is a book published yearly with information about the weather, sun, moon, and many other things of general interest.
2 **Bifocals** are eyeglasses with one lens for reading and another for seeing at a distance.
3 On July 4, 1776, the thirteen English colonies declared their independence from England. The War of Independence began the year before.

I. Comprehension

Answer these questions about the story. Use your own ideas to answer the questions marked with a check ✔.

Paragraph 1

   1. Benjamin Franklin went to school for only two years. Why?
   2. What were his teachers?

Paragraph 2

✔ 3. Franklin didn't get along with his brother, but he liked the printing business. Do you think his love of reading helped him to like his work as a printer? Explain your answer.
   4. What did he do at the age of 17?

Paragraph 3

   5. How did Franklin prove that lightning is electricity?
   6. Name three things he invented.
✔ 7. He never accepted a penny for his inventions. What does that tell us about him?

Paragraph 4

   8. Name three things Franklin organized or started in Philadelphia.

Paragraph 5

   9. How long did Franklin spend in London? What did he do there?
  10. What did he do in 1775?

Paragraph 6

  11. What did Franklin persuade the king and other French officials to do?
  12. What was his opinion about war and peace?

II. Key Words

Before studying these words, reread the story and try to guess their meaning.

Nouns		Verbs	Irregular Pasts	Adjectives
candle	lightning	get along	had - have	several
printer	rod	publish	hit - hit	postal
publisher	stove	experiment (+n.)	got - get	
apprentice	relation	prove	let - let	**Other**
success	declaration	invent	won - win	even (adv.)
scientist	independence	organize		against (prep.)
inventor	minister (+v.)	lend		
invention	popularity	pave		
kite	official	represent		
electricity	opinion	maintain		

III. Story Completion

Complete the story with these words.

proved	opinion	get along	kite	even
organize	success	invented	candles	published

Printer, Scientist, Inventor, Patriot

Benjamin Franklin was the fifteenth of 17 children and helped

his father make _____. His older brother

James was a printer and Ben worked for him for several years,

but they didn't _____. His brother

_____ hit him, so Ben ran away to

Philadelphia.

In Philadelphia, Franklin _____ a

newspaper and a famous almanac. The almanac was a great

_____.

Franklin was also a scientist with a special interest in electricity.

He _____ that lightning was electricity by

flying a _____ in a lightning storm. He also

_____ a stove, lightning rods, and bifocals.

Franklin helped _____ the first hospital and

the first fire department in Philadelphia and did many other things

to improve the city.

During the War of Independence, Franklin was the United

States' Minister to France and helped obtain French aid for his

country. Later he helped arrange peace with England. In his

_____ , there never was a good war or a bad

peace.

IV. Dialogs

Key Words

Nouns		Verbs		Adjectives	Other
saying	string	collect	get = understand	clearer	worth (prep.)
prevention	widow	attach	worry (+n.)	dangerous	
cure (+v.)		attract			

An Ounce of Prevention

In 1732, Franklin first published *Poor Richard's Almanack*. In it were many sayings. A saying expresses an important truth in a few words. Franklin meets Ann at a party, and they're talking about his almanac.

Complete the dialog with these words.

collect   **pound**   **sayings**   **clearer**   **remember**

Ann: What's the name of your almanack?

Ben: *Poor Richard's Almanack.*

Ann: Is that the one with all those _____?

Ben: Yes, people love them and they _____ them too.

Ann: Where do you get them?

Ben: From my reading. Some people _____ stamps.

Ann: And you collect sayings.

Ben: Exactly, but I rewrite many of them.

Ann: Why?

Ben: To make them _____. Do you want to hear one?

Ann: Sure.

Ben: An ounce of prevention is worth a _____ of cure.

Ann: That's a good one. I like it.

Be Careful, Ben!

Ben is preparing a kite that he's going to fly to test his idea that lightning is electricity. His wife Debbie is afraid he may hurt himself.

Complete the dialog with these words.

attract	dangerous	attaching	widow	string

Debbie: What are you doing with that piece of metal?

Ben: I'm _____ it to the kite.

Debbie: What for?

Ben: So the kite will _____ lightning.

Debbie: Do you want to kill yourself?

Ben: No, I want to prove something.

Debbie: What?

Ben: That lightning is electricity.

Debbie: And what are you doing with that key?

Ben: I'm tying it to the end of this _____.

Debbie: I don't get it.

Ben: After the lightning hits the metal, it'll go down the string and into the key.

Debbie: Isn't that _____?

Ben: A little.

Debbie: Be careful, Ben! I don't want to be a _____!

Ben: Don't worry! I will.

V. Sharing ideas

Discuss these questions in pairs or small groups.

1. Franklin came from a large family. How many brothers and sisters do you have?
2. Why is staying in school more important today than in the time of Franklin?
3. Why were candles so important when Franklin lived?
4. Do you like to read? What do you like to read? Do you read much?
5. Do you like to read books and articles about science?
6. Franklin started the first lending library in America. Is it easy to get a public library card? Do you have to pay to get one? Do you have one?
7. Almanacs are still popular. What's in them? Have a student borrow one from the library and bring it to class.
8. Franklin said, "There never was a good war or a bad peace." Do you agree? Explain your answer.

VI. Books You May Enjoy

1. Greene, Carol. *Benjamin Franklin: A Man with Many Jobs.* A Rookie Biography. Chicago: Childrens Press, 1988. 48 pp. (Level 1)

2. Scarf, Maggi. *Meet Benjamin Franklin.* Set-up Paperback Books. New York: Random House, 1989. 64 pp. (Level 1)

3. Graves, Charles P. *Benjamin Franklin: Man of Ideas.* A Discovery Book. Champaign, Illinois: Gerrard Publishing Company, 1960. 70 pp. (Level 1).

4. Fritz, Jean. *What's the Big Idea, Ben Franklin?* New York: Coward-McCann, Inc., 1976. 48 pp. (Level 2)

5. Davidson, Margaret. *The Story of Benjamin Franklin, Amazing American.* A Dell Yearling Biography. New York: Dell Publishing, 1988. 92 pp. (Level 2)

An Introduction to the
Declaration of Independence

On June 11, 1776, the Continental Congress appointed a committee of five including Thomas Jefferson, Benjamin Franklin, and John Adams to prepare a statement declaring that the thirteen American colonies were independent of England and explaining why. The committee asked Jefferson to write this declaration of independence because he was an excellent writer. Jefferson wrote the declaration in a house on Market Street in Philadelphia. The committee reviewed it, and Jefferson made some changes in it.

Congress made a few more changes in the Declaration of Independence, and all of the states except New York approved it on July 4, 1776. This was the birth of the United States of America. Eleven days later, New York also approved the Declaration.

Sections of the
Declaration of Independence

When in the course of human events, it becomes necessary for one people to dissolve the political bands which have connected them with another, ... they should declare the causes which impel them to the separation.

We hold these truths to be self-evident, that all men are created equal, that they are endowed by their Creator with certain inalienable rights, that among these are life, liberty, and the pursuit of happiness.... The history of the present King of Great Britain is a history of repeated injuries....

We, therefore, the Representatives of the United States of America, ... do, in the name, and by authority of the good people of these Colonies, solemnly publish and declare, that these United Colonies are, and of right ought to be free and independent States; ... And ... with a firm reliance on the protection of Divine Providence, we mutually pledge to each other our lives, our fortunes, and our sacred honor.

Vocabulary Notes

Paragraph 1

1. **course:** movement; passing
2. **dissolve:** to end
3. **bands:** material used to hold something together
4. **connect:** to unite
5. **impel:** to cause; to force

Paragraph 2

6. **self-evident:** immediately clear
7. **endow:** to give
8. **inalienable:** that which can not be taken away
9. **pursuit:** the act of trying to obtain something
10. **injury:** harm or damage

Paragraph 3

11. **solemn(ly):** very serious(ly)
12. **firm:** strong; unchanging
13. **reliance:** dependence
14. **Divine Providence:** God's loving care
15. **mutual:** having in common
16. **pledge:** to make a solemn promise

5 George Washington

Washington Crossing the Delaware River

Important Events

February 22, 1732	Washington is born in Virginia
January 6, 1759	Marries Martha Custis
June 15, 1775	Is appointed Commander of the Continental Army
October 1781	Defeats English at Yorktown, Virginia to win the Revolutionary War
May 25, 1787	Is elected President of the Constitutional Convention
February 4, 1789	Is elected President of the United States
December 14, 1799	Dies at Mount Vernon, Virginia at the age of 67

Preview

1. George Washington, the first President of the United States, chose very good people to help him run the government. Many say this is a President's most important job. Do you agree? Explain your answer.

2. In 1775, the War of Independence between the thirteen English colonies and England began. It was a long and difficult war and ended in 1781. Since then, the United States and England have been friends most of the time. And we're close friends today. Why?

George Washington
(1732 – 1799)

George Washington was the first President of the United States, but sometimes he wondered how it happened. He wasn't much of a public speaker; he didn't like political battles and parties; he was quiet. But he understood and liked people and knew how to get them to work together. He was always fair, and everyone respected and trusted him. He was from the South, and he was also popular in the North.

Washington was born on February 22, 1732 in Virginia. Math was his favorite subject and he was very good at it. However, his father died when he was 11, and he didn't have the opportunity to go to college.

Washington was six feet three, strong, and athletic. He loved to swim, to hunt, and, above all, to ride horses. He was one of the best horsemen in all of Virginia. He also liked to dance and go to parties.

With his love of math and the outdoors, it wasn't surprising that Washington became a surveyor. But when he was 20, he joined the Virginia militia and fought for Virginia and England against the French who had settled in the Ohio Valley. The French put four bullet holes in his coat and shot two horses from under him. He became a war hero and learned a lot about military affairs. That was why, in 1775, the colonies made him a general and the Commander of the Continental Army.

The thirteen English colonies declared their independence from England on July 4, 1776, but the War of Independence began the year before at Lexington and Concord, Massachusetts. It was a terrible war. England was a rich country with a large, powerful army and navy. The United States was a poor country with a small, weak army and no navy. Its soldiers didn't have enough food, shoes, or guns. They lost many battles, but they finally won the war because they refused to quit. They knew they had to fight hard to protect their country, freedom, and independence. They also had a lot of help from France and some from Spain.

After the war, Washington was happy to return to his wife Martha and their large farm at Mount Vernon in Virginia. He was a successful farmer from 1784 to 1787 and hoped to remain at Mount Vernon. But in 1787,

George Washington

he became a member and then president of the convention that wrote the Constitution of the United States. And in 1789, he was elected the first President of the United States, his greatest honor and most difficult job.

Washington served eight years as President before retiring to Mount Vernon in 1797. He died two years later at Mount Vernon on December 17, 1799. In the words of General Henry Lee, "He was first in war, first in peace, first in the hearts of his countrymen."

I. Comprehension

Answer these questions about the story. Use your own ideas to answer the questions marked with a check ✔.

Paragraph 1

1. Washington sometimes wondered how he became President. Why did he wonder?
2. Name three good things about Washington.

Paragraph 2

3. What was Washington's favorite subject?
✔ 4. Why do you think his father's death made it difficult for him to go to college?

Paragraph 3

5. Name five activities that he liked.

Paragraph 4

6. What did Washington become because of his love of math and the outdoors?
7. Why did the colonies make him a general and Commander of the Continental Army?

Paragraph 5

8. Compare the English and American armies and navies.
9. Give two reasons why America won the war.
✔ 10. Was the War of Independence more important to the United States or to England? Explain your answer.

Paragraph 6

11. What did Washington do after the War of Independence?

Paragraph 7

12. How long did Washington serve as President?

II. Key Words

Before studying these words, reread the story and try to guess their meaning.

Nouns		Verbs	Irregular Pasts	Adjectives
party (+v.)	commander	wonder (+n.)	understood - understand	fair
opportunity	bullet	respect (+n.)	fought - fight	athletic
outdoors	affairs	hunt (+n.)	put - put	surprising
surveyor	convention	join	shot - shoot	terrible
militia	constitution	refuse	began - begin	powerful
		quit	lost - lose	weak
		retire		successful

Other

however
(conj., adv.)
above all
(idiom)

III. Story Completion

Complete the story with these words.

successful	hunt	fair	convention	fought
weak	wondered	affairs	athletic	refused

Commander of the Colonial Army
and First President

Sometimes Washington _____ how he became the President of the United States. He didn't like political parties or battles, but he was _____ to everyone and very popular both in the North and the South.

Washington was six three, strong, and _____. He liked to swim, ride horses, and _____.

When he was 20, he _____ for Virginia and England against the French and learned a lot about military _____.

Washington was the Commander of the Continental Army in the War of Independence against England. The English Army was large and powerful. The Continental Army was small and _____, but the Americans won the war because they _____ to quit.

After the war, Washington returned to his farm at Mount Vernon. He was a _____ farmer from 1784 to 1787. In 1787, he was elected president of the _____ that wrote the Constitution of the United States, and in 1789, was elected the first President of the United States.

IV. Dialogs

Key Words

Nouns		Verbs	Adjectives	Other
troops	dawn (+v)	desert	discouraged	badly (adv.)
blanket	influence (+v.)	consider	brilliant	ahead (adv.)
		accomplish	stronger	

We Need a Victory

After a bad defeat in New York City, Washington and his army retreated across New Jersey into Pennsylvania. On December 26, 1776, Washington recrossed the Delaware River and won a big victory at Trenton, New Jersey. Colonel Henry Knox was one of his closest aides.

Complete the dialog with these words.

discouraged   brilliant   cross   badly   dawn

Washington: We need a victory _____ .

Henry Knox: I know. The troops are _____ .

Washington: And some are deserting.

Henry Knox: Many don't have shoes or blankets.

Washington: We have to attack.

Henry Knox: Are you thinking of attacking the Hessians* at Trenton?

Washington: Yes. We'll _____ the Delaware tonight after midnight.

Henry Knox: But it's Christmas Day.

Washington: Exactly, and their troops are busy eating and drinking.

Henry Knox: And tomorrow morning they'll be sleeping.

Washington: Right, and we'll attack at _____ .

Henry Knox: A _____ move.

* England paid Hessian soldiers to fight for them in America during the War of Independence. The Hessians came from Hesse, which is now part of Germany.

Our Government is Weak

After the Revolution ended in 1781, it became clear that the United States needed a stronger central government. In 1787, the states met in Philadelphia to consider the problem. They decided to write a new constitution. Washington is talking to his wife Martha about the problem.

Complete the dialog with these words.

stronger   **influence**   **meeting**   **accomplish**   **consider**

George: I have some good news and some bad news.

Martha: Give me the good news first.

George: There's going to be an important _____ in Philadelphia.

Martha: Why?

George: To _____ a new constitution for the country.

Martha: Does that mean you're going to Philadelphia again?

George: Yes, that's the bad news.

Martha: Do they really need you?

George: Yes, I can have a big _____ .

Martha: But what do you hope to _____ ?

George: To make our government _____ . It's very weak.

Martha: Are you sure?

George: Yes, we can't go on this way. We have to do something.

Martha: I didn't know it was that bad. Go ahead and good luck!

V. Sharing Ideas

Discuss these questions in pairs or small groups.

1. What was or is your favorite subject in school?
2. Can you swim? Do you swim much? Are you a good swimmer?
3. Do you like to dance? Do you dance much?

4. Why do you think it was difficult for the thirteen colonies to work and fight together?

5. Why do you think Washington is called the Father of the United States? Try to give three reasons.

6. What do you think was the main reason why France and Spain helped the colonists?

   a. They liked them and their ideas.

   b. They didn't like England.

7. Name some places and things that are named after Washington.

8. If you're from another country, does your country have a hero or heroes similar to Washington? Who?

VI. Books You May Enjoy

1. Miller, Frances A. *George Washington*. Biographies from American History. Belmont, California: Fearon-Janus, 1989. 32 pp. (Level 1)

2. Brandt, Keith. *George Washington*. Mahwah, New Jersey: Troll Associates, 1985. 30 pp. (Level 1)

3. Sabin, Francene. *American Revolution*. Mahwah, New Jersey: Troll Associates, 1985. 30 pp. (Level 1)

4. Graff, Stewart. *George Washington, Father of Freedom*. A Discovery Book. Champaign, Illinois: Garrard Publishing Company, 1964. 80 pp. (Level 1)

5. Milton, Joyce. *The Story of George Washington, Quiet Hero*. A Dell Yearling Biography. New York: Dell Publishing, 1988. 92 pp. (Level 2)

The Constitutional Convention
(May–September 1787)

After the colonies won the War of Independence, the United States was governed by the Articles of Confederation. The central government under the Articles was very weak. To strengthen the government, a constitutional convention met in Philadelphia from May 25, 1787 to September 17, 1787. The Convention planned to revise the Articles of Confederation, but instead replaced them with a new Constitution.

The new Constitution consisted of a preamble, or introduction, and seven articles. The articles provided for a Senate and a House of Representatives to make laws, a President to enforce the laws, and a Supreme Court to interpret the laws.

Beginning of the Constitution

The new Constitution went into effect on June 21, 1787 and was eventually ratified by all thirteen states. In 1791, ten amendments were added to the Constitution. These amendments are called the Bill of Rights because they protect individual rights.

Vocabulary Notes

1. **revise:** to change
2. **preamble:** introduction
3. **enforce the law:** to make sure that the law is obeyed
4. **interpret:** to explain
5. **ratify:** to approve
6. **amendment:** addition

Sections of the Constitution of the United States
Preamble

We the people of the United States, in order to form a more perfect Union, establish justice, insure domestic tranquility, provide for the common defence, promote the general welfare, and secure the blessings of liberty to ourselves and our posterity, do ordain and establish this CONSTITUTION for the United States of America.

Article I

Section 1. All legislative powers herein granted shall be vested in a Congress of the United States, which shall consist of a Senate and a House of Representatives.

Article II

Section 1. The executive power shall be vested in a President of the United States of America. He shall hold office during the term of four years, . . .

Article III

Section 1. The judicial power of the United States shall be vested in one Supreme Court, and in such inferior courts as the Congress may from time to time ordain and establish.

Amendment I

Congress shall make no law respecting an establishment of religion, or prohibiting the free exercise thereof; or abridging the freedom of speech, or of the press; or of the right of people peaceably to assemble, and to petition the government for a redress of grievances.

Vocabulary Notes

Preamble

1. **insure:** to make sure that
2. **domestic:** having to do with one's own country; not foreign
3. **tranquility:** peace
4. **defence:** in 1887, **defense** was spelled **defence**
5. **promote:** to help something to grow
6. **welfare:** well-being
7. **secure:** to obtain
8. **posterity:** those who will live in the future; those who will live after us
9. **ordain:** to decree

Article I

10. **legislative:** having to do with the law
11. **herein:** in this (Constitution)
12. **grant:** to give
13. **vest:** to give power or authority to

Article II

14. **executive:** having to do with managing a company or carrying out the laws of a country
15. **term:** limited amount of time

Article III

16. **judicial:** having to do with judges or a court of law
17. **inferior:** less important

Amendment I

18. **respecting:** (preposition) about; with respect to
19. **prohibit:** to say something can't be done; to forbid by law
20. **thereof:** of it
21. **abridge:** to make less; to lessen
22. **assemble:** to come together as a group
23. **petition:** to ask the government for something formally and in writing
24. **redress:** correction
25. **grievances:** a wrong that causes a person to complain

6 Abigail Adams

Abigail Adams

Important Events

November 11, 1744	Abigail Smith is born in Weymouth, Massachusetts
October 25, 1764	Abigail marries John Adams
1765–1772	Abigail, John Quincy, Susanna, Charles, and Thomas are born
June 1784	Abigail sails for Europe to join John in Paris
November 1796	John Adams is elected President
October 28, 1818	Abigail dies in Quincy, Massachusetts
November 1824	John Quincy Adams is elected President

Preview

1. Abigail Adams, the wife of the second President of the United States, wanted women to have more educational opportunities. Do you think that women today have the same educational opportunities as men? Has Abigail Adams's wish come true?

2. Abigail Adams and her husband were separated for almost ten years while he was serving his country in Philadelphia and Europe. As a result, she became a great letter writer. How often do you write personal letters? Do most people today use the phone instead of writing letters? Do you?

Abigail Smith Adams
(1744–1818)

Abigail Smith was born in a small town just south of Boston on November 11, 1744. Abigail was sickly as a child and never went to school. But her father, who was a Protestant minister, taught her to read and write, and she educated herself. Her father's library was her favorite room, and reading was her favorite occupation.

When Abigail was 17, she and John Adams fell in love. He was a lawyer and graduate of Harvard College. At first, her parents didn't think he was good enough for her, but that didn't stop Abigail and John. They waited until she was almost 20 and got married on October 25, 1764. Adams was delighted to marry a woman who liked to read, think, and discuss politics. He listened carefully to her ideas, and she listened carefully to his. They shared easily.

After their marriage, Abigail and John lived on a small farm in Braintree, Massachusetts, and he practiced law in Boston. They had five children, Abigail, John Quincy, Charles, Thomas, and Susanna, who died as an infant. Love of God, family, and country were the most important things in Abigail's life, but she was more than a loving wife and mother. She believed strongly in education for women at a time when few did. She was probably the first to lobby[1] for women's rights, asking her husband and other lawmakers in Philadelphia "to remember the ladies. Be more generous and favorable to them than your ancestors."

Abigail and John were early supporters of independence for the American colonies. From 1774 to 1784, he was away most of the time serving his country, first in Philadelphia and later in Europe. Abigail quickly learned to manage the farm and family finances, and she raised and taught their children. She also became a great letter writer, for that was the only way to keep in contact with her husband. Finally, in 1784, she went to live with him in Paris and then in London, when he was appointed the first United States' Ambassador to England.

John Adams

John Quincy Adams

Abigail was happy to return to Braintree in 1788—by then the part of Braintree she lived in was called Quincy. In 1789, John Adams was elected the first Vice President of the United States. He served under President Washington, and Martha Washington and Abigail Adams became good friends. In 1796, Adams was elected the second President of the United States, and Abigail and John were the first ones to live in the new White House in Washington, D.C.

Abigail and John's oldest son, John Quincy, a lawyer and a graduate of Harvard, was elected to the U.S. Senate in 1803. In 1817, he was appointed Secretary of State. Abigail and John were very proud of him.

Abigail Adams died in Quincy, Massachusetts on October 28, 1818. Six years later, John Quincy Adams was elected the sixth President of the United States. Abigail Adams is the only woman in history who had both a husband and a son serve as President of the United States.

[1] To **lobby** is to try to influence a lawmaker to vote for what you want.

The White House

I. Comprehension

Answer these questions about the story. Use your own ideas to answer questions marked with a check ✔.

Paragraph 1

    1. Why didn't Abigail Smith go to school?

    2. Who taught her to read and write?

Paragraph 2

    3. What was John Adams?

    4. How did he feel about the fact that Abigail Adams liked to read, think, and discuss politics?

Paragraph 3

    5. How many children did Abigail and John have? What happened to Susanna?

    6. What was Abigail Adams probably the first to do?

Paragraph 4

7. What did Abigail learn to do when John was in Philadelphia?

✔ 8. Do you think she was an independent person? Explain your answer.

Paragraph 5

✔ 9. Abigail's experience as the wife of John Adams, the U.S. Ambassador to England, made it easier for her when he was elected Vice President of the United States. How?

10. Where were Abigail and John the first ones to live?

Paragraph 6

11. Name two important political positions John Quincy Adams held before becoming President of the United States.

Paragraph 7

12. What is true of Abigail Adams that is true of no other woman in history?

II. Key Words

Before studying these words, reread the story and try to guess their meaning.

Nouns		Verbs	Irregular Pasts	Adjectives
minister (+v.)	ancestor	delight (+n.)	taught - teach	sickly
occupation	supporter	share (+n.)	fell (in love) - fall	generous
graduate (+v.)	finance (+v.)	believe		favorable
politics	ambassador	lobby (+n.)		proud
lawmaker	vice president	manage		
secretary of state		raise (+n.)		**Other**
		appoint		enough
				(adv., adj.)

III. Story Completion

Complete the story with these words.

finances	delighted	lawmakers	shared	appointed
taught	supporters	occupation	raise	lobby

Remember the Ladies

Abigail Smith never went to school, but her father

_____ her to read, and reading was her

favorite _____.

Abigail fell in love with John Adams, but her parents didn't

think he was good enough to marry her. But that didn't stop

Abigail and John from getting married in 1764. He was

_____ to marry a woman who liked to read

and discuss politics. They _____ easily.

Abigail Adams believed strongly in the education of women and

was probably the first to _____ for women's

rights. She asked her husband and the other _____

in Philadelphia "to remember the ladies."

Abigail and John were early _____ of

independence for the American colonies and, from 1774 to 1784,

he served his country in Philadelphia and Europe. Abigail quickly

learned to manage the family _____ and had

to _____ the children by herself.

Abigail and John's first son, John Quincy Adams, was elected to

the U.S. Senate in 1803 and _____ Secretary

of State in 1817. They were very proud of him.

IV. Dialogs

Key Words

Nouns	Verbs	Adjectives
permission	respect (+n.)	lucky
Continental Congress	got - past of get	bright
mission	miss (+n.)	
support (+v.)		

In Love

Abigail is telling Elizabeth Smith, her aunt, that she's in love with John Adams. Abigail's family calls Abigail, Nabby.

Complete the dialog with these words.

bright　　　　**permission**　　　　**lucky**　　　　**respects**　　　　**graduate**

Nabby:　I'm so happy today.

Aunt:　Are you in love, Nabby?

Nabby:　Yes, I am.

Aunt:　And who's the _____ man?

Nabby:　John Adams. He's a Harvard _____.

Aunt:　He must be _____.

Nabby:　Yes and he _____ my ideas.

Aunt:　Does he want to marry you?

Nabby:　Yes, he does.

Aunt:　Did he ask your father's _____?

Nabby:　Not yet. He's asking him tonight.

Aunt:　Your father will need time to think about it.

Nabby:　That's okay. We can wait.

Aunt:　Of course. You're very young.

A Letter from Congress

In November 1777, John Adams received a letter from the Continental Congress asking him to go to France to work with Benjamin Franklin to get French help for the United States in its War of Independence.

Complete the dialog with these words.

support   **win**   **mission**   **have to**   **got**

John: I have a letter from Congress.

Abigail: What does it say?

John: They want me to go to France on a special _____.

Abigail: Can you tell me what it is?

John: Yes, to help Ben Franklin win French _____.

Abigail: But you just _____ back from Philadelphia three weeks ago.

John: I know, but we need French help to _____ the war.

Abigail: How long will you be there?

John: Maybe a year or two. I'm not sure.

Abigail: I'll miss you so much, but I understand.

John: And I'll miss you too, but I _____ go.

V. Sharing Ideas

Discuss these questions in pairs or small groups.

1. When Abigail Smith was a girl, women didn't receive much formal education. Why not?
2. Abigail studied French when she was a girl. How did that help her later in life?
3. What is your first language? What other languages have you studied or are you studying?
4. History was Abigail's favorite subject. Do you like to study history? Do you like to read history books?

5. What is the value of studying history?

6. Abigail married a person who shared her interests. How important to a happy marriage is sharing interests? Explain your answer.

7. Abigail and John Adams communicated well. How important to a happy marriage is good communication? Explain your answer.

8. John Adams sacrificed much to serve his country. Do you think this was a love of country, or a love of politics and a desire to have an important job? Or both? Explain your answer.

VI. Books You May Enjoy

1. Sabin, Francene. *Young Abigail Adams*. Mahwah, New Jersey: Troll Associates, 1992. 48 pp. (Level 1)

2. Peterson, Helen Stone. *Abigail Adams: "Dear Partner."* A Discovery Book. Champaign, Illinois: Garrard Publishing Company, 1967. 80 pp. (Level 1)

3. Holberg, Ruth Langland. *Abigail Adams*. Real People. Evanston, Illinois: Row, Peterson, and Company, 1950. 36 pp. (Level 1)

4. Kelly, Regina Z. *Abigail Adams: The President's Lady*. Piper Books. Boston: Houghton Mifflin, 1962. 185 pp. (Level 2)

5. Wagoner, Jean Brown. *Abigail Adams: Girl of Colonial Days*. Indianapolis, Indiana: Bobbs Merrill Company, Inc., 1962. 200 pp. (Level 2)

3

Leaders of a Growing Country

7 Thomas Jefferson

Thomas Jefferson Writing the Declaration of Independence

Important Events

April 13, 1743	Jefferson is born in Shadwell, Virginia
1762	Graduates from William and Mary College
January 1, 1772	Marries Martha Skelton
June 1776	Writes the Declaration of Independence
1797–1801	Serves as Vice President of the United States
1801–1809	Serves as President of the United States
July 4, 1826	Dies at Monticello on the fiftieth anniversary of the Declaration of Independence

Preview

1. When Thomas Jefferson was President, he wanted to stay close to the people, to listen to the ordinary person. Do you think that's easy for a President? Is it possible?

2. In 1992, William Clinton was elected President of the United States. Did you know that his middle name is Jefferson? And that he rode a bus 70 miles from Monticello, Jefferson's home in Virginia, to Washington, D.C., the day he became President? Like Jefferson, Clinton promised to be the President of the ordinary person.

Thomas Jefferson
(1743–1826)

Thomas Jefferson was born on a farm in Shadwell, Virginia on April 13, 1743. He was always an excellent student, frequently studied 14 hours a day, and loved to read. But he also loved to fish, hunt, ride horses, and play the violin. He graduated from William and Mary College in 1762. Then he studied law. He was a person of many interests and occupations. He was a farmer, a lawyer, a writer, a scientist, an inventor, an architect, the President of the United States, and the founder of the University of Virginia.

In 1772, Jefferson married Martha Skelton, a pretty 23-year-old widow. She loved music, as Jefferson did, and was well educated. They had six children, but only their daughters Martha and Maria lived to be adults. Jefferson's wife died at Monticello in 1782. She was only 34 years old. For months, he did nothing but mourn her loss.

Jefferson had a 35-room home on a mountain near Charlottesville, Virginia. He called his home Monticello, an Italian word that means "little mountain." He made all the plans for it himself and carefully supervised its construction. It was very beautiful and he was proud of it.

In June 1776, Jefferson wrote the Declaration of Independence in Philadelphia. A committee that included Benjamin Franklin and John Adams reviewed it, and Congress made a few changes in it, but Jefferson was its main author. It begins by saying that "all men are created equal" and have the right to "life, liberty, and the pursuit[1] of happiness." Then it declares that the American colonies are free and independent of England.

In 1800, Jefferson was elected the third President of the United States. Before his election, he complained that the President was acting too much like a king. Since Jefferson believed in equality, he changed all that. There were round tables and no special places at White House dinners. Jefferson dressed like an ordinary citizen. When newspapers criticized him, he wasn't happy, but he didn't say or do anything. He wanted newspapers to feel free to criticize the President. He was a man of the people. He listened

Monticello

to the workers, to the small businessmen, and, above all, to the farmers. He felt they were the heart of America.

In 1803, the United States purchased the Louisiana Territory from France for 15 million dollars. Now that was a lot of money, but at about four cents an acre, it was a real bargain. It doubled the size of the United States and was one of the great accomplishments of Jefferson's Presidency.

In 1809, Jefferson completed his second term as President and was happy to return to Monticello. Here he enjoyed his 12 grandchildren, farmed, wrote letters, and received numerous visitors. He spent six years on his final great achievement, the founding of the University of Virginia in nearby Charlottesville. Thomas Jefferson died at Monticello on July 4, 1826, the fiftieth anniversary of the signing of the Declaration of Independence.

[1] **Pursuit** is the act of trying to get something, for example, "the *pursuit* of money."

I. Comprehension

Answer these questions about the story. Use your own ideas to answer the questions marked with a check ✔.

Paragraph 1

1. Jefferson loved to study and to read. What else did he love to do?
2. What did he do after he graduated from William and Mary College?

Paragraph 2

3. Give three reasons why Jefferson married Martha Skelton.
✔ 4. When she died, Jefferson was only 39, but he said he would never marry again and he never did. Why do you think he made this decision?

Paragraph 3

5. What did Jefferson call his home? What does "monticello" mean in Italian?

Paragraph 4

6. The Declaration of Independence says that all men have three rights. What are they?
7. What does it declare about the thirteen American colonies?

Paragraph 5

8. Why did Jefferson use round tables at White House dinners and dress like an ordinary citizen?
✔ 9. Jefferson thought farmers were the heart of the nation, and he wanted the United States to be a nation of farmers. Why do you think he felt that way?

Paragraph 6

10. How much did the Louisiana Territory cost the United States per acre?

Paragraph 7

11. What was Jefferson's last great achievement?
12. When did Jefferson die? What was special about this date?

II. Key Words

Before studying these words, reread the story and try to guess their meaning.

Nouns		Verbs		Adjectives
violin	election	mourn	complain	main
interest (+v.)	citizen	supervise	criticize	equal (+v., n.)
architect	acre	create	purchase (+n.)	ordinary
founder	bargain (+v.)	declare	double (+adj.)	numerous
loss	accomplishment			nearby (+adv.)
construction	presidency			
author	term			
pursuit	achievement			

III. Story Completion

Complete the story with these words.

bargain	complained	interests	criticize	main
citizen	purchased	equal	mourn	doubled

A Man of Many Occupations

Thomas Jefferson was a man of many _____

and occupations. He was a farmer, lawyer, writer, inventor, and

architect.

His wife Martha died when she was only 34. He did nothing for

months, but _____ her death.

Jefferson was the _____ author of the

Declaration of Independence, which he wrote in 1776. It declares

that "all men are created _____" and have the

right to "life, liberty, and the pursuit of happiness."

In 1800, Jefferson was elected the third President of the United

States. Before his election, he _____ that the

President was acting too much like a king. Jefferson, however,

believed in equality and dressed like an ordinary _____.

He also felt that newspapers should be free to _____

the President.

In 1803, the United States _____ the

Louisiana Territory from France for 15 million dollars. At about

four cents an acre, it was a _____ and one

of the great accomplishments of Jefferson's Presidency. It

_____ the size of the United States.

IV. Dialogs

Key Words

Nouns		Verbs	Adjectives
point (+v.)	debt	spend	basic
press	middle class	reduce	federal
			common

What About the Rights of Women?

It's 1776, and a reporter is asking Jefferson about The Declaration of Independence.

Complete the dialog with these words.

pursuit   **point**   **still**   **means**   **created**

Reporter: You write that all men are _____ equal.

Jefferson: Yes, that's what I believe.

Reporter: But some men are smarter than others.

Jefferson: Very true, but they're _____ equal.

Reporter: How?

Jefferson: We all have the same basic rights.

Reporter: What basic rights?

Jefferson: The right to life, liberty, and the _____ of happiness.

Reporter: You say all men are created equal. What about women?

Jefferson: All "men" _____ all men and women.

Reporter: Then you should say that.

Jefferson: You have a _____.

The Farmer and the Common Man

It's 1800, and a reporter is asking Jefferson about his plans to run for President. Jefferson is running against John Adams, the second President of the United States.

Complete the dialog with these words.

business	federal	press	reduce	debt

Reporter: If you become President, what will you do?

Jefferson: Give more freedom to the _____ and the people.

Reporter: And what else?

Jefferson: I'll cut taxes.

Reporter: Does that mean less spending?

Jefferson: Exactly. The _____ government is too big.

Reporter: And what about the national _____?

Jefferson: I'll _____ it.

Reporter: Do you think that John Adams is for the rich?

Jefferson: Yes, and for big _____.

Reporter: And who are you for?

Jefferson: The small farmer and the common man. The middle class.

Reporter: Do you think you'll win?

Jefferson: Of course! There are more middle-class people than rich ones.

V. Sharing Ideas

Discuss these questions in pairs or small groups.

1. Jefferson was very intelligent and had many talents, but he was not a good public speaker. Why would this make it difficult for him to be elected President today?
2. Jefferson had a large personal library. What kind of books, do you think, were in his library?
3. Jefferson loved to ride horses and was good at it. Why was riding horses so important in those days?
4. Did you ever ride a horse? Did you like riding?
5. In what way are all people equal?
6. In what ways are people unequal? For example, some people are stronger than others.
7. All "men" are created equal means all men and women are created equal. But did women in the United States have the right to vote in 1776? Did they have the same job opportunities as men? Explain your answer.
8. Newspapers and people in the United States feel free to criticize the President. Do you think that's good? Explain your answer.

VI. Books You May Enjoy

1. Smith, Kathie Billingslea. *Thomas Jefferson.* The Great American Series. New York: Simon & Schuster, 1988. 24 pp. (Level 1)
2. Barrett, Marvin. *Meet Thomas Jefferson.* Step-up Paperback Books. New York: Random House, 1989. 72 pp. (Level 1)
3. Colver, Anne. *Thomas Jefferson: Author of Independence.* A Discovery Book. Champaign, Illinois: Garrard Publishing Company, 1963. 80 pp. (Level 1)
4. Hargrove, Jim. *Thomas Jefferson: Third President of the United States.* Encyclopedia of Presidents. Chicago: Childrens Press, 1986. 100 pp. (Level 2)
5. Crisman, Ruth. *Thomas Jefferson: Man with a Vision.* Scholastic Biography. New York: Scholastic, Inc., 1992. 152 pp. (Level 2)

8 Lewis and Clark

Meriwether Lewis

William Clark

Important Events

August 18, 1774	Meriwether Lewis is born in Virginia
May 2, 1803	The Louisiana Purchase is signed in Paris
May 14, 1804	The Lewis and Clark Expedition leaves St. Louis
Oct. 1804 – April 1805	The expedition spends the winter in North Dakota
November 7, 1805	The expedition sights the Pacific Ocean
September 23, 1806	The expedition returns to St. Louis

Preview

1. Imagine that you are going on a 3,500 mile trip from St. Louis to the Pacific Ocean with a group of friends or classmates. It's 1804 and there are no stores and no roads on the way. You have to travel by boat and by foot. What would you take with you?

2. Imagine you and your friends are taking the same trip today. You still have to travel by boat and by foot, but you can take anything you wish. What would you take?

The Lewis and Clark Expedition
(1804 – 1806)

Meriwether Lewis was born near Charlottesville, Virginia on August 18, 1774. For two years he was the personal secretary of his friend Thomas Jefferson, the President of the United States. Before that, he served in the United States Army for 12 years. One day the President told him he had a special mission for him.

Jefferson asked Lewis to lead an expedition to explore the Louisiana Territory,[1] cross the Rocky Mountains, and go all the way to the Pacific Ocean. The President wanted him to find a waterway from the Mississippi to the Pacific and to make friends of the Native Americans he met. He was also to make detailed maps and to describe the rivers, mountains, plants, and animals he saw.

Lewis chose his close friend Captain Bill Clark to be the co-leader of the expedition. Like himself, Captain Clark was in the army for many years, loved the outdoors, and had a lot of experience with Native Americans. However, the two men were also very different. Lewis was quiet, serious, and liked to be alone. Clark liked to talk and joke, and was always friendly.

About forty men and Lewis's dog Seaman[2] left St. Louis on May 14, 1804. Most of the men were soldiers, and they were called the Corps of Discovery. They traveled northwest up the muddy Missouri River in three boats loaded with food and gifts for the Native Americans. In October, they reached Mandan, North Dakota, where they built a fort among friendly Native Americans and stayed for the winter.

In April 1805, the Corps of Discovery started west from Mandan with three new members, a French trapper named Charbonneau, his Native American wife, Sacagawea, and their baby. They reached the beginning of the Missouri River and the Rocky Mountains in July. With the help of Sacagawea, they bought horses from the Native Americans, crossed the Rocky Mountains, and continued along the Snake and Columbia Rivers. On November 7, 1805, they sighted their goal, the Pacific Ocean!

In March 1806, the Corps started their long journey back to St. Louis and arrived there on September 23, 1806, tired but very happy. They had accomplished everything President Jefferson wanted except to find a

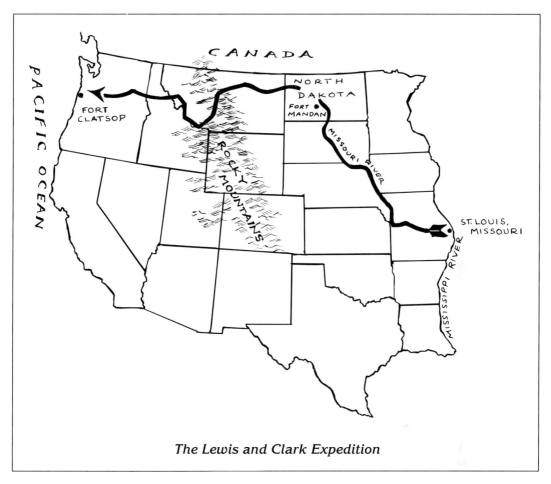

The Lewis and Clark Expedition

waterway to the Pacific. But it wasn't easy. They had to contend with grizzly bears, mosquitoes, and rattlesnakes. They came close to starving and had to eat horses, dogs, and roots. They suffered from the heat and the cold, from too much rain, and from heavy snow. But they were the first explorers to cross the North American Continent north of Mexico, and the expedition was a great success.

1 In 1803, the United States purchased the Louisiana Territory from France for 15 million dollars.
2 Seaman was a large Newfoundland dog. He was a good hunter and watchdog. Most books call him Scannon, but a recent study shows his real name was Seaman.

I. Comprehension

Answer these questions about the story. Use your own ideas to answer the questions marked with a check ✔.

Paragraph 1

1. What important job did Lewis have for two years?

Paragraph 2

2. What did Jefferson ask Lewis to do?
3. What did Jefferson want him to do when he met Native Americans?

Paragraph 3

4. What did Lewis and Clark have in common?
5. How were they different?

Paragraph 4

✔ 6. Why do you think Lewis took his dog on the expedition?
✔ 7. Do you think it was a good idea that the leaders of the expedition and most of the men were soldiers? Explain your answer.
8. What did they do when they reached Mandan, North Dakota?

Paragraph 5

9. Who were the three new members of the expedition?
10. How did the expedition cross the Rocky Mountains?

Paragraph 6

11. What did the Corps of Discovery fail to do?
12. Why did they have to eat dogs and roots?

II. Key Words

Before studying these words, reread the story and try to guess their meaning.

Nouns		Verbs	Irregular Pasts	Adjectives
mission	fort	joke (+n.)	told - tell	detailed
expedition	trapper	sight (+n.)	left - leave	close
waterway	goal	accomplish	built - build	muddy
co-leader	grizzly bear	contend		loaded
outdoors	rattlesnake	starve		
experience (+v.)	root			**Other**
Corps of Discovery				among (prep.)
				along (prep., adv.)
				except (prep.)

III. Story Completion

Complete the story with these words.

goal   chose   roots   among   mission

contend   detailed   left   except   experience

A Difficult Journey

One day President Jefferson asked his personal secretary, Meriwether Lewis, to go on a special _____. He asked him to lead an expedition of soldiers from St. Louis to the Pacific Ocean. He wanted them to make _____ maps of the area and describe everything they saw.

Lewis _____ his friend Captain Bill Clark to be their co-leader. Clark was in the army for many years and had a lot of _____ with Native Americans.

They _____ St. Louis in May 1804 and, in October, reached Mandan, North Dakota, where they built a fort _____ friendly Native Americans. In the spring of 1805, they continued their journey, crossed the Rocky Mountains and, on November 7, 1805, sighted their _____ , the Pacific Ocean.

They did everything the President asked _____ to find a waterway to the Pacific. But it was a difficult trip. They had to _____ with grizzly bears, mosquitoes, and rattlesnakes. They almost starved and had to eat horses, dogs, and _____.

IV. Dialogs

Key Words

Nouns		Verbs	Other
challenge (+v.)	hut	observe	so far (idiom)
climate	journal	hunt (+n.)	
route	hostility		
puddle	appendicitis		

A Special Job

President Jefferson is talking to his secretary Meriwether Lewis. He wants him to lead an expedition to the Pacific Ocean.

Complete the dialog with these words.

route   climate   observe   challenge   find

Jefferson: I have a special job for you, Meriwether.

Lewis: What is it, Mr. President?

Jefferson: I want you to lead an expedition to the Pacific Ocean.

Lewis: That's some _____!

Jefferson: I know, but you can do it.

Lewis: I'll try, Sir.

Jefferson: I want you to do three things.

Lewis: What are they?

Jefferson: _____ a waterway to the Pacific.

Lewis: Good. That would give us a short _____ to China.

Jefferson: Exactly. I also want you to make friends of the Native Americans you meet.

Lewis: Fine. I know them well from my army days.

Jefferson: And I want you to write down everything you

_____.

Lewis: You mean about the plants and animals.

Jefferson: Yes, and about the rivers, the mountains, and the

_____.

A Fort and Some Huts

It's October and the Lewis and Clark Expedition is in North Dakota, where the Mandan Native Americans live. The weather is getting cold.

Complete the dialog with these words.

journal   puddle   hostility   so far   hunt

Lewis: This morning I saw some ice in a _____.

Clark: So did I. It's time to find a place to stay for the winter.

Lewis: We'll build a fort and some huts here near the Mandan Native Americans.

Clark: Good. The men need rest and time to _____.

Lewis: And we need time to prepare our reports for President Jefferson.

Clark: That's right. I have a lot of work to do on my maps and

_____.

Lewis: How far are we from St. Louis?

Clark: About 1,600 miles.

Lewis: We've been lucky _____.

Clark: Except for the death of Sergeant Floyd from appendicitis.

Lewis: And the _____ of the Teton Sioux.

Clark: Yes, we almost had to fight them.

Lewis: But they finally let us pass.

V. Sharing Ideas

Discuss these questions in pairs or small groups.

1. Lewis and Clark were very different. Do you think that people who are very different frequently become good friends?
2. Why couldn't the Lewis and Clark Expedition travel in the winter?
3. Name some of the dangers the Corps of Discovery faced.
4. The expedition could not bring enough food for such a long journey. How do you think the men got more food?
5. When the Native Americans saw Lewis and Clark and their men, how do you think they felt? Happy? Afraid? Surprised? Curious?
6. The Lewis and Clark Expedition was good for the United States. Do you think it was good or bad for the Native Americans who lived in the Louisiana Territory? Explain your answer.
7. How were the explorations of Lewis and Clark and Samuel de Champlain similar?
8. Do you like to hike in the woods to explore and enjoy nature? Do you do it much?

VI. Books You May Enjoy

1. Stein, R. Conrad. *The Story of the Lewis and Clark Expedition*. Cornerstones of Freedom Series. Chicago: Childrens Press, 1978. 31 pp. (Level 1)

2. Montgomery, Elizabeth Rider. *Lewis and Clark*. World Explorers. Champaign, Illinois: Garrard Publishing Company, 1966. 96 pp. (Level 1)

3. Lacy, Don. *The Lewis and Clark Expedition, 1804–06: The Journey That Opened the American Northwest*. A Focus Book. New York: Franklin Watts, Inc., 1974. 89 pp. (Level 2)

4. McGrath, Patrick. *The Lewis And Clark Expedition*. Turning Points in American History. Morristown, New Jersey: Silver Burdett Company, 1985. 63 pp. (Level 2)

5. Blumberg, Rhoda. *The Incredible Journey of Lewis and Clark*. New York: Lothrop, Lee & Shepard Books, 1987. 143 pp. (Level 2)

9 Sacagawea

Sacagawea, Lewis, and Clark Crossing the Rocky Mountains

Important Events

1788 (?)	Sacagawea is born
February 11, 1805	Her son, Pomp, is born
April 7, 1805	Sacagawea, Pomp, and Charbonneau leave Fort Mandan with Lewis and Clark
August 17, 1805	Sacagawea is reunited with her brother Cameahwait
August 14, 1806	Sacagawea returns to Mandan with Lewis and Clark
1812 or 1884	Sacagawea dies

Preview

1. Lewis and Clark were happy to have Sacagawea join the Corps of Discovery because she knew the Shoshoni language and could help them get the horses they needed to cross the Rocky Mountains. She was also better than anyone at finding wild fruit and vegetables. Why?

2. Sacagawea had to travel about 2,000 miles from Fort Mandan to the Pacific Ocean and another 2,000 miles to get back. Her baby Pomp was less than two months old when they left Fort Mandan. How dangerous was this trip for the baby? Explain your answer.

Sacagawea
(1788?–1812 or 1884)

Sacagawea was a Shoshoni Native American, and her tribe lived in the Rocky Mountains, where she was born around 1788. A terrible thing happened to Sacagawea when she was 12. She was on a hunting expedition with her family and tribe, when Minnetaree Native Americans surrounded and attacked their camp. She tried to escape, but one of their warriors captured her and made her his slave. He took her back to North Dakota, where she spent long hours working in the cornfields and cooking. Then one day a French-Canadian trapper[1] by the name of Charbonneau bought her and made her his wife.

In October 1804, the Corps of Discovery, led by Lewis and Clark, arrived in North Dakota. Sacagawea's husband asked to join their expedition to the Pacific as a guide and interpreter. Lewis and Clark hired him and said that Sacagawea could come too. They were happy to have her because they knew that she was a Shoshoni and could help them get horses from her tribe, and she was happy to have a chance to see her people and land again.

Sacagawea was pregnant at the time and, in February 1805, gave birth to her son Jean Baptiste. She called him Pomp, which means leader or chief in Shoshoni. She asked to take Pomp with her on the expedition, and Lewis and Clark said okay.

Sacagawea was able to help the Corps of Discovery in many ways. One day a sudden wind hit the boat she was in and almost turned it over. Her husband was steering the boat and panicked, but Sacagawea stayed calm and risked her life to save some very important supplies and papers. Lewis and Clark were very grateful. She was also better than anyone at finding wild fruit and vegetables. And her presence and Pomp's helped the Corps make peace with many of the Native American tribes they met. When they got to the Rockies, she helped obtain from the Shoshoni the horses the Corps needed to cross the mountains.

Sacagawea Greeting her Brother Cameahwait

You can imagine how happy and surprised Sacagawea was when she discovered that her brother Cameahwait was still alive and was the chief of the Shoshoni. However, she decided to stay with her husband and the Corps when it came time for them to leave the Shoshoni and to continue their journey to the Pacific.

The Corps finally reached the Pacific in November 1805. Pomp got sick on the return trip, but Captain Clark treated him and he recovered. Clark was very fond of Pomp and called him a "beautiful promising child." He even offered to take him back to St. Louis to raise and educate him, and eventually he did. But, at the time, Pomp was too young to leave Sacagawea. In August 1806, the Corps arrived back in Mandan, North Dakota. When the Corps continued on to St. Louis, Sacagawea, Pomp, and Charbonneau remained in Mandan.

Not much is known of the rest of Sacagawea's life, but it seems that she died on December 12, 1812 of a fever; she was about 25. Some, however, think she returned to her tribe and lived to be almost 100. In any case, Sacagawea was a brave woman who contributed much to the success of one of the greatest expeditions in U.S. history.

1 A **trapper** is a person who catches (traps) animals to get their skins.

I. Comprehension

Answer these questions about the story. Use your own ideas to answer questions marked with a check ✔.

Paragraph 1
1. What happened to Sacagawea when she was 12?
2. What was Charbonneau? What did he do?

Paragraph 2
3. What did Charbonneau ask Lewis and Clark?
4. Why were they happy to have Sacagawea go with them?

Paragraph 3
5. What made it difficult for Sacagawea to go on the expedition?

Paragraph 4
6. What did Sacagawea do when her husband panicked?
✔ 7. How do you think her presence and Pomp's helped the Corps make peace with many of the Native American tribes?

Paragraph 5
8. What did Sacagawea discover about her brother Cameahwait?
✔ 9. Why do you think she decided to leave the Shoshoni and stay with Charbonneau and the Corps of Discovery?

Paragraph 6
10. What happened to Pomp on the return trip? Who treated him?
11. What did Captain Clark offer to do?

Paragraph 7
12. When and how did Sacagawea probably die? How old was she?

II. Key Words

Before studying these words, reread the story and try to guess their meaning.

Nouns		Verbs		Adjectives	
warrior	interpreter	surround	panic (+n.)	pregnant	wild
slave (+v.)	wind	escape (+n.)	risk (+n.)	sudden	surprised
cornfields	return (+v.)	capture (+n.)	treat	calm	fond (of)
trapper	rest	turn over	recover	better	promising
	case	steer	contribute		

Other

eventually (adv.)

III. Story Completion

Complete the story with these words.

sudden	hired	wild	steering	slave
fond	risked	pregnant	interpreter	surrounded

Helping the Corps of Discovery

When Sacagawea was 12, Minnetaree Native Americans

_____ and attacked the hunting party she was

with. One of the Minnetaree warriors captured her and made her

his _____.

A French-Canadian trapper by the name of Charbonneau

bought her and married her. Lewis and Clark _____

Charbonneau as a guide and _____.

Sacagawea was _____ at the time, but she

too wanted to go with Lewis and Clark, and they were happy to

have her.

Sacagawea helped the Corps of Discovery in many ways. One

day a _____ wind hit the boat she was in.

Charbonneau was _____ and panicked, but she remained calm and _____ her life to save some important papers and supplies. She was also very good at finding _____ fruit and vegetables. And she helped the Corps of Discovery get the horses they needed to cross the Rockies.

Sacagawea brought her baby Pomp with her on the trip, and Captain Clark became _____ of the baby and even offered to educate him. But, at the time, Pomp was too young to leave Sacagawea.

IV. Dialogs

Key Words

Nouns	Verbs	Adjectives		Other
guide (+v.)	join	wonderful	such (a)	rarely (adv.)
	worry (+n.)	tough	healthy	

What About the Baby?

Charbonneau asks Lewis and Clark if he can go with the Corps of Discovery. They decide to take him and Sacagawea. She's very happy.

Complete the dialog with these words.

tough   **worry**   **joining**   **healthy**   **wonderful**

Sacagawea: Did you ask Lewis and Clark about _____ the expedition?

Charbonneau: Yes, just now.

Sacagawea: Well, what did they say?

Charbonneau: Okay, and you can go too.

Sacagawea: That's _____! Now I can see my people again.

Charbonneau: It's going to be a long, _____ trip.

Sacagawea: I know, but I'm young and _____.

Charbonneau: You're also pregnant. What are you going to do with the baby?

Sacagawea: I'll take the baby with me.

Charbonneau: Isn't that dangerous?

Sacagawea: Don't _____. I'll take good care of the baby.

Charbonneau: Okay.

It's So Good to See You Again!

When Sacagawea returned to her people, she had an emotional reunion with her brother Cameahwait. He asks her what Lewis and Clark want.

Complete the dialog with these words.

such a	return	proud	guide	dead

Sacagawea: It's so good to see you again!

Cameahwait: And I'm so happy to see you!

Sacagawea: I was afraid you were _____.

Cameahwait: Pomp looks a lot like you. You must be

_____ of him.

Sacagawea: Very. He's _____ good baby. He rarely cries.

Cameahwait: And what do Lewis and Clark want from us?

Sacagawea: Horses and a _____.

Cameahwait: We can give both. But we want something in

_____.

Sacagawea:	I'll talk to Captain Clark. He's very friendly.
Cameahwait:	And what about Captain Lewis?
Sacagawea:	He's nice too, but he's quiet and very serious.
Cameahwait:	Are you going to stay with us?
Sacagawea:	I don't know. I'll have to think about that.

V. Sharing Ideas

Discuss these questions in pairs or small groups.

1. What do you think Charbonneau's first language was? Explain your answer.
2. Do you think that he helped take care of Pomp? Explain your answer.
3. Many Native Americans died from sicknesses they got from the European settlers. Their bodies had no resistance to these sicknesses. Why not?
4. The Native Americans were unable to defend themselves against the European settlers because they didn't have guns. What did the Native Americans generally use to defend themselves?
5. Are there still many Native Americans living in the United States? Where do they live?
6. Sacagawea missed her people and land. How did you feel when you first came to the United States?
7. Do you still miss your first country?
8. Did you ever go back to visit your country? If so, tell us about your trip.

VI. Books You May Enjoy

1. Blassingame, Wyatt. *Sacagawea: Indian Guide.* Discovery Book. Champaign, Illinois: Garrard Publishing Company, 1965. 80 pp. (Level 1)

2. Burt, Oliver, *Sacajawea.* A Visual Biography. New York: Franklin Watts, Inc., 1978. 57 pp. (Level 2)

3. Rowland, Della. *The Story of Sacajawea, Guide to Lewis and Clark.* A Dell Yearling Biography. New York: Dell Publishing, 1989. 92 pp. (Level 2)

4. Skold, Betty W. *Sacagawea: The Story of an American Indian.* Minneapolis, Minnesota: Dillon Press, Inc., 1977. 74 pp. (Level 2)

4

Civil War Leaders

10 Abraham Lincoln

Abraham Lincoln

Important Events

February 12, 1809	Lincoln is born in Kentucky
September 9, 1836	Receives license to practice law
November 4, 1842	Marries Mary Todd in Springfield, Illinois
November 6, 1860	Is elected sixteenth President of the United States
April 12, 1861	Civil War begins at Fort Sumter, South Carolina
April 9, 1865	Civil War ends at Appomattox Court House, Virginia
April 14, 1865	Lincoln is shot at Ford's Theatre
April 15, 1865	Dies in Washington, D.C. at the age of 56

Preview

1. Young Abraham Lincoln was poor, but this did not keep him from becoming the sixteenth President of the United States. Do you think the United States is still a land of opportunity for the poor? Explain your answer.

2. President Lincoln's biggest problem was the Civil War between the North and the South. Today there are still civil wars between groups or sections of some countries. Can you name one of these countries?

Abraham Lincoln
(1809–1865)

Abraham Lincoln was born in a log cabin in the woods of Kentucky on February 12, 1809. His father was a farmer and a carpenter. When Abe was seven, the family moved to Indiana, where his mother died when he was nine.

Lincoln spent most of his youth plowing, milking cows, and chopping wood, but what he really liked to do was read. A biography of George Washington was one of his favorites, and he loved to read the Bible and Shakespeare. Lincoln went to school for less than a year, but he educated himself by reading.

When Lincoln was 22, he moved to New Salem, Illinois, where he became a store clerk. He was six feet four inches tall, an excellent wrestler, and the best story teller in town. He was so honest that people called him "Honest Abe." Lincoln was very popular and an excellent public speaker, so it was natural that he turned to politics.

Lincoln was elected to the state legislature four times in a row, and studied law. In 1836, he became a lawyer and the following year moved to Springfield, the capital of Illinois, where he married Mary Todd in 1842. Lincoln was elected to Congress in 1846 and, in 1858, he ran for the U.S. Senate and lost. However, in 1860, Abraham Lincoln was elected the sixteenth President of the United States.

It was a very difficult time to be President. Slavery and the right of a state to leave the Union, to secede, were the two big issues. In the South, whites owned almost four million African Americans. Most of these slaves worked on large cotton plantations.[1] Lincoln considered slavery a moral and social evil and was always opposed to its spread to new states, but he felt that the Constitution allowed Southern states to have slaves.

Seven Southern states seceded from the Union after Lincoln's election, and four more joined them later. As President of the United States, Lincoln felt strongly that he couldn't allow that. When the South attacked Fort Sumter in South Carolina, a bloody civil war began in which brothers killed brothers. The Northern states, the Union, fought to restore the unity of the country. The Southern states, the Confederacy, fought to be a separate country and keep their slaves. On January 1, 1863, Lincoln issued the Emancipation Proclamation[2] freeing all the slaves held in Confederate territory. This was the first step in abolishing all slavery.[3] The Civil War finally came to an end on April 9, 1865. It lasted four years, much longer than anyone expected, and many brave soldiers on both sides lost their lives.[4] But the Union was saved and slavery was ended.

On Friday, April 14, just five days after the end of the Civil War, Lincoln and his wife went to see a play at Ford's Theatre in Washington, D.C. During the play, a well-known actor, by the name of John Wilkes Booth, shot Lincoln. The doctors did all they could, but Abraham Lincoln died at 7:22 AM on April 15 at the age of 56. When Lincoln took office, the Northern and Southern states were hopelessly divided, and almost four million Americans were slaves. When President Lincoln died, the states were preparing to reunite, and all Americans were free. The United States was again one nation and guaranteed liberty to all.

[1] A **plantation** is a large farm that grows cotton or tobacco. They were common in the South.
[2] **To emancipate** is to free. A **proclamation** is an official public announcement.
[3] The **Emancipation Proclamation** didn't abolish slavery in the border states loyal to the Union. It was the Thirteenth Amendment to the Constitution, passed on January 31, 1865, that abolished all slavery in the United States. Lincoln pushed hard to get this amendment passed.
[4] More than 620,000 soldiers lost their lives in the Civil War — 360,000 from the North and 260,000 from the South.

I. Comprehension

Answer these questions about the story. Use your own ideas to answer the questions with a check ✔.

Paragraph 1

1. Where was Lincoln born? What was his father?

Paragraph 2

2. What did Lincoln spend most of his youth doing?

✔ 3. Lincoln went to school for less than a year. Why do you think he spent so little time in school?

Paragraph 3

4. Why was it natural that Lincoln turned to politics?

Paragraph 4

✔ 5. Why would a lawyer want to live in the state capital?

6. What happened to Lincoln in the election of 1858? And in the election of 1860?

Paragraph 5

   7. What were the two big issues Lincoln had to face when he became President?

   8. What did Lincoln think of slavery?

Paragraph 6

   9. Why did the Northern states fight?

  10. Why did the Southern states fight?

Paragraph 7

  11. When was Lincoln shot? And where? When did he die?

  12. What was the situation in the United States when Lincoln took office? And what was it when he died?

II. Key Words

Before studying these words, reread the story and try to guess their meaning.

Nouns			Verbs		Adjectives
log cabin	(in a) row	plantation	plow (+n.)	restore	honest
woods	legislature	spread (+v.)	milk (+n.)	abolish	moral
youth	senate	unity	chop	reunite	civil (war)
biography	issue (+v.)	Emancipation	secede	guarantee (+n.)	well-known
clerk	slavery	Proclamation	oppose		
wrestler	evil	territory			**Other**
		play (+v.)	**Irregular Pasts**		hopelessly adv.)
			felt - feel		

III. Story Completion

Complete the story with these words.

restore	in a row	plowing	issues	abolishing
evil	woods	lost	spread	wrestler

The Sixteenth President of the United States

    Abraham Lincoln was born in the _____ of

Kentucky on February 12, 1809. When he was young, he spent

most of his time _____ , milking cows, and chopping wood, but what he really liked to do was read.

Lincoln was six feet four inches tall, an excellent _____ , and a great story teller.

Lincoln was elected to the state legislature four times _____ and, in 1836, became a lawyer. In 1858, he ran for the U.S. Senate and _____ , but two years later he was elected the sixteenth President of the United States.

The new President faced two big _____ , slavery and the right of states to leave the Union. Lincoln con-sidered slavery a moral and social _____ and opposed its _____ to new states.

Eleven Southern states left the Union and fought the Civil War to become a separate country. The Northern states fought to _____ the unity of the nation. On January 1, 1863, Lincoln issued the Emancipation Proclamation, freeing all the slaves held in Confederate territory, the first step in _____ all slavery in the United States.

IV. Dialogs

Key Words

Nouns		Verbs	Adjective	Other
secession	sense (+v.)	face (+n.)	major	absolutely (adv.)
concern (+v.)	humor (+v.)	allow		

Saving the Union and Ending Slavery

Lincoln became President in April 1861. His biggest problem was how to reunite the country. He also wanted to end slavery. He's talking to a reporter.

Complete the dialog with these words.

wrong	face	concern	reunite	allow

Reporter: What are the biggest problems you _____ , Mr. President?

Lincoln: Secession and slavery, especially secession.

Reporter: So your first goal is to _____ the country.

Lincoln: Absolutely. We must save the Union. That's my major

_____.

Reporter: And what about slavery?

Lincoln: It's _____. Morally, socially, and politically.

Reporter: How are you going to end it?

Lincoln: For now, I plan to limit it to the states that already

_____ it.

Reporter: But shouldn't the federal government abolish slavery in the South?

Lincoln: I don't think it has that power.

Reporter: But when and how is slavery going to end?

Lincoln: I'm not sure, but it'll happen. We need time.

Willie is Very Sick

Lincoln had four sons, Robert, Edward, William, and Thomas or Tad. Edward died as a baby. Robert went to Harvard to study, and Willie and Tad lived in the White House. Lincoln is talking to his secretary Nicolay.

Complete the dialog with these words.

so	humor	upset	just	smart

Nicolay: How's the family, Mr. Lincoln?

Lincoln: I have some bad news. Willie is very sick.

Nicolay: What's the problem?

Lincoln: The doctors aren't sure. It may be typhoid fever.

Nicolay: That's too bad. Mrs. Lincoln must be very _____.

Lincoln: Terribly, and so am I.

Nicolay: Willie is so friendly and he's _____ , too.

Lincoln: Yes, and he has a wonderful sense of _____.
We're very close.

Nicolay: I know. He's _____ like you, Mr. President.

Lincoln: I hope and pray he gets better soon.

Nicolay: _____ do I. And how's Tad?

Lincoln: He's okay, but he's worried about his brother.*

* Willie died in the White House on February 20, 1862 at the age of 11. His loss caused great sorrow to Lincoln and his wife, who never fully recovered from the shock.

V. Sharing Ideas

Discuss these questions in pairs or small groups.

1. Lincoln was an honest politician. Do you think most politicians are honest?

2. Lincoln liked to speak before groups, to speak in public. Do you?

3. Lincoln was also a great story teller. Why was telling stories more popular in 1850 than today? Do you like to tell stories? Are you good at it?

4. Today everyone sees that slavery is wrong. Why do you think that there were many in 1860, especially in the South, who didn't see that?

5. The Southern states that left the Union felt they had a right to secede. Do you think they did? Explain your answer.

6. Name some places and things that are named after Lincoln.

7. Did you ever visit the Lincoln Memorial in Washington, D.C.? If so, tell us about it.

8. Reread the story about Washington and compare Lincoln and Washington. How were they alike? Who was more into farming? Who was from a poor family? Who was a better public speaker? Who was more popular when he was President?

VI. Books You May Enjoy

1. Brains, Rae. *Abraham Lincoln.* Mahwah, New Jersey: Troll Associates, 1985. 30 pp. (Level 1)

2. Bledsoe, Lucy Jane. *Abraham Lincoln.* Biographies from American History. Belmont, California: Fearon-Janus, 1989. 32 pp. (Level 1)

3. Cary, Barbara. *Meet Abraham Lincoln.* Set-up Books. New York: Random House, 1965. 86 pp. (Level 1)

*4. Freedman, Russell. *Lincoln: A Photobiography.* New York: Clarion Books, 1987. 150 pp. (Level 3)

* Books with an asterisk are for teachers. They are too difficult for students using *Leaders of the Americas.*

The Battle of Gettysburg
(July 1–3, 1863)

From July 1 to July 3, 1863, the most important battle of the Civil War took place at Gettysburg, Pennsylvania. The North won the battle, the turning point of the Civil War. Thousands of Confederate and Union soldiers died in the battle. After the battle, the Confederate dead were returned to the South, and the Union dead were buried in a special cemetery in Gettysburg.

The Gettysburg cemetery was dedicated on November 19, 1863. The main speaker at the dedication was Edward Everett. He spoke for almost two hours. Then President Abraham Lincoln spoke for just a few minutes. But it was Lincoln's speech that became famous, probably the most famous speech in the history of the United States. In a few words, Lincoln explained the purpose of the Civil War and praised the brave soldiers who had died in the battle of Gettysburg.

> that this nation under God shall have a new birth of freedom, and that
>
> government of the people, by the people, for the people, shall not perish from the earth.

Ending of the Gettysburg Address

The Gettysburg Address
(November 19, 1863)

"Fourscore and seven years ago our fathers brought forth on this continent a new nation conceived in liberty and dedicated to the proposition that all men are created equal.

Now we are engaged in a great civil war testing whether that nation, or any nation so conceived and so dedicated, can long endure. We are met on a great battlefield of that war. We have come to dedicate a portion of that field as a final resting place for those who here gave their lives that that nation might live. It is altogether fitting and proper that we should do this.

But, in a larger sense, we cannot dedicate, we cannot consecrate, we cannot hallow this ground. The brave men, living and dead, who struggled here have consecrated it far above our poor power to add or detract. The world will little note nor long remember what we say here, but it can never forget what they did here. It is for us the living rather to be dedicated here to the unfinished work which they who fought here have thus far so nobly advanced.

It is rather for us to be here dedicated to the great task remaining before us — that from these honored dead we take increased devotion to that cause for which they gave the last full measure of devotion — that we here highly resolve that these dead shall not have died in vain, that this nation under God shall have a new birth of freedom, and that government of the people, by the people, for the people shall not perish from the earth."

Vocabulary Notes

Paragraph 1

1. **fourscore:** score means 20; fourscore = 80
2. **fathers:** the leaders of the United States when it became an independent country; for example, Franklin, Washington, Jefferson, John Adams.
3. **bring forth:** to create; to give birth to
4. **conceive:** to form an idea; to become pregnant
5. **proposition:** idea; statement

Paragraph 2

6. **be engaged:** to be occupied
7. **endure:** to last
8. **portion:** part
9. **fitting:** right

Paragraph 3

10. **consecrate:** to make sacred
11. **hallow:** to make holy
12. **struggle:** to fight
13. **detract:** to make less
14. **thus far:** up to now

Paragraph 4

15. **task:** job
16. **resolve:** to decide or determine
17. **in vain:** without purpose; uselessly
18. **perish:** to die

11 Robert E. Lee

Robert E. Lee on his Horse Traveller

Important Events

January 19, 1807	Robert E. Lee is born in Stratford Hall in Virginia
June 1829	Graduates with high honors from West Point
June 30, 1831	Marries Mary Anne Custis at Arlington, Virginia
June 1, 1862	Takes command of the Army of Northern Virginia
April 9, 1865	Surrenders at Appomattox Court House
October 2, 1865	Becomes president of Washington College
October 12, 1870	Dies in Lexington, Virginia

Preview

1. Robert E. Lee was a graduate of West Point, the special military school where the United States educates and trains its army officers. What qualities does a man or woman need to be a good officer, a good military leader? For example, they have to be brave.

2. Robert E. Lee was more loyal to the state of Virginia than to the United States. Today things are different. Americans often move from state to state, travel more, and communicate quickly and easily. Why has this made us less loyal to the states in which we live and more loyal to our country?

Robert E. Lee
(1807–1870)

Robert E. Lee was born in Stratford Hall in Virginia on January 19, 1807. His father, "Lighthorse Harry" Lee, was a brilliant cavalry leader and a hero in the War of Independence. Lee's father later became the Governor of Virginia.

Lee grew up in Alexandria, Virginia. Math was his favorite subject, and swimming and riding horses were his favorite activities. He wanted to be a soldier like his father, so he applied to the U.S. Military Academy at West Point, New York and was accepted.

He studied hard at West Point and graduated second in a class of 46. In his four years there, he never received a single demerit.[1] After graduation, he entered the Army Corps of Engineers. Two years later, on June 30, 1831, he married Mary Anne Custis, the great granddaughter of Martha Washington. They had seven children.

In the war between the United States and Mexico in 1846–1847, Lee was a scout and aide of General Winfield Scott, who praised him for his skill and bravery in battle. In 1852, he was appointed superintendent of the Military Academy at West Point. That was a great honor, and he improved the course of studies and discipline in his three years there.

In the beginning of 1861, Lee was called to Washington after seven Southern states seceded from the Union. He didn't favor secession and he believed slavery was wrong. But when President Lincoln offered him the field command of the Union Army, he didn't accept the honor. He felt he couldn't lead an army against Virginia, his family, and his people.

Three days after Virginia seceded from the Union, Lee resigned from the United States Army with much regret. He felt it was his duty to defend Virginia. In June 1862, he was put in charge of the Confederate Army of Northern Virginia. The North had more soldiers and supplies, but Lee's army won victory after victory because of his leadership and the courage and spirit of his soldiers.

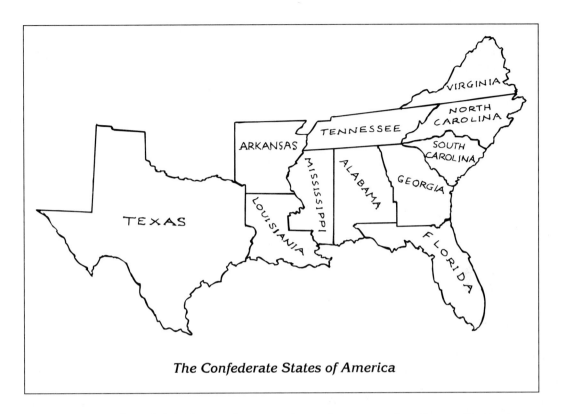

The Confederate States of America

Then, in July of 1863, Lee's army lost the great battle at Gettysburg, Pennsylvania. That was the turning point of the war. Lee's soldiers didn't have enough to eat and many didn't have shoes to wear. They fought on bravely, but the North, under General Ulysses Grant, captured Richmond, the capital of the Confederacy, and the situation of the Confederate forces was hopeless. On April 9, 1865, Robert E. Lee met Ulysses S. Grant at Appomattox Court House in Virginia. Lee surrendered and the Civil War was over. After the war, Lee became the president of Washington College in Lexington, Virginia. He died in Lexington on October 12, 1870.

[1] A **demerit** is a negative mark a person receives for doing something wrong.

I. Comprehension

Answer these questions about the story. Use your own ideas to answer the questions marked with a check ✔*.*

Paragraph 1

1. Why was Robert E. Lee's father famous?

Paragraph 2

2. What was Lee's favorite subject? And his favorite activities?
✔ 3. Why were swimming and riding good preparation for his life in the army?

Paragraph 3

4. How do we know that Lee was a good student?
5. What did he do two years after his graduation from West Point?

Paragraph 4

6. Why did General Winfield Scott praise Lee?
7. What did Lee improve at West Point?

Paragraph 5

8. How did Lee feel about slavery?
9. Why didn't he accept the field command of the Union Army?

Paragraph 6

✔ 10. Why do you think Lee resigned with much regret?
11. Why did Lee's army win victory after victory? Give two reasons.

Paragraph 7

12. What was the turning point of the Civil War?

II. Key Words

Before studying these words, reread the story and try to guess their meaning.

Nouns			Verbs	Adjectives
cavalry	aide	spirit	apply	single
governor	skill	courage	praise (+n.)	great
demerit	superintendent	leadership	appoint	(granddaughter)
corps	discipline (+v.)	turning point	resign	hopeless
engineer	regret (+v.)	situation	surrender (+n.)	(be) over
scout (+v.)	duty			

Irregular Pasts	Other
grew (up) - grow	against (prep.)
	in charge of (prep.)

III. Story Completion

Complete the story with these words.

praised	in charge of	appointed	turning point	against
grew up	regret	surrendered	duty	applied

Skill and Bravery in Battle

Robert E. Lee was born in January 1807 and _____ in Alexandria, Virginia. He loved to swim and ride horses, and math was his favorite subject. He wanted to be a soldier, so he _____ to the U.S. Military Academy at West Point, New York and was accepted.

Lee was a scout and aide of General Scott in the war between the United States and Mexico. Scott _____ him for his skill and bravery in battle. In 1852, he was _____ superintendent of the Military Academy at West Point.

Lincoln offered Lee the field command of the U.S. Army, but he couldn't lead an army _____ Virginia and his people. He resigned from the army with much _____ . He felt it was his _____ to defend Virginia.

In June 1862, Lee was put _____ the Army of Northern Virginia. He won many victories, but he lost the great battle of Gettysburg, the _____ of the war. On April 9, 1865, Lee _____ to General Grant at Appomattox Court House in Virginia, ending the Civil War.

IV. Dialogs

Key Words

Nouns		Verb	Irregular Past	Adverbs
commander	offer (+v.)	represent	let - let	highly
judge (+v.)				frankly

An Honor I Can't Accept

Francis Blair was a good friend and adviser of Abraham Lincoln. Lincoln asked him to meet with Lee and offer him the field command of the Union Army. The two men met at Blair's home in Washington on April 18, 1861.

Complete the dialog with these words.

resign   **highly**   **lead**   **mean**   **commander**

Blair: I'm Mr. Blair. It's nice to meet you, Colonel Lee.

Lee: And I'm pleased to meet you, Sir.

Blair: President Lincoln thinks very _____ of you.

Lee: That's nice to hear.

Blair: And he wants to make you the field _____ of the Union Army.

Lee: I'm sorry, I can't accept the honor.

Blair: Why not, Colonel?

Lee: I can't _____ an army against Virginia.

Blair: But you're an officer in the U.S. Army.

Lee: If Virginia leaves the Union, I'll have to _____ from the army.

Blair: Does that _____ you'll fight against the Union?

Lee: I certainly don't want to.

Blair: But what if the Union attacks Virginia?

Lee: My duty will be to defend Virginia.

President of Washington College

After the Civil War, Lee intended to buy a small farm. But in August 1865, Washington College of Lexington, Virginia asked him to become its president. Lee served as president of the college until he died in 1870. After his death, the college was renamed Washington and Lee. Lee is talking to a judge who represents Washington College.

Complete the dialog with these words.

let   **frankly**   **represent**   **consider**   **enough**

Judge: General Lee, I'm Judge John Brockenbrough of Lexington, Virginia.

Lee: Pleased to meet you, Judge. Have a chair.

Judge: Thank you. I _____ Washington College, and I have an offer for you.

Lee: What is it?

Judge: We want you to become the president of Washington College.

Lee: _____ , I was thinking of buying a small farm to live on, but . . .

Judge: We can't offer you much money. Only $1,500 a year.

Lee: That's okay. I just want _____ to live on.

Judge: And we have a house and garden for you and your family.

Lee: What about my horse Traveller?

Judge: We have a place for him, too. We know how much he means to you.

Lee: Well, nothing is more important to the South than good schools.

Judge: So you'll _____ our offer.

Lee: Of course. And I'll _____ you know in a few weeks.

V. Sharing Ideas

Discuss these questions in pairs or small groups.

1. Math was Lee's favorite subject. Do you like math? Are you good at it?
2. Where is West Point? What do you know about its training?
3. It wasn't so easy for Lee to get into West Point. Do you think it's easy or difficult to get into West Point today? What does a person need to get in?
4. Does West Point accept women? Did it accept women in Lee's day?
5. The Army Corps of Engineers was probably very happy to have Lee. Why?
6. What states of the United States were part of Mexico before the Mexican-American War?
7. Do you think Lee's duty was to defend Virginia? Or was it his duty to stay in the U.S. Army? Explain your answer.
8. At 58, Lee became the president of Washington College. What experience did he have that prepared him for this job?

VI. Books You May Enjoy

1. Bains, Rae. *Robert E. Lee: Brave Leader*. Mahwah, New Jersey: Troll Associates, 1968. 48 pp. (Level 1)

2. Graves, Charles P. *Robert E. Lee: Hero of the South*. Discovery Book. Champaign, Illinois: Garrard Publishing Company, 1964. 80 pp. (Level 1)

3. Grant, Matthew G. *Robert E. Lee: The South's Great General*. War Heroes of America. Mankato, Minnesota: Creative Education, 1974. 31 pp. (Level 1)

4. Solem, Elizabeth K. *Robert E. Lee*. Real People. Evanston, Illinois: Row, Peterson and Company, 1950. 36 pp. (Level 2)

5. Vinton, Iris. *The Story of Robert E. Lee*. Signature Books. New York: Grosset & Dunlap, 1952. 182 pp. (Level 2)

12 Clara Barton

Clara Barton Taking Care of a Wounded Soldier on the Battlefield

Important Events

December 25, 1821	Clara Barton is born in North Oxford, Massachusetts
May 1839	Begins 15 years of teaching
1854	Starts work in the U.S. Patent Office
July 11, 1862	Receives permission to serve on battlefields
1881	Founds the American Red Cross
1881–1904	Serves as president of the American Red Cross
April 12, 1912	Dies in Glen Echo, Maryland at the age of 91

Preview

1. Teachers and nurses do very different work, but both teachers and nurses help others. Clara Barton was a great teacher and a great nurse. She loved to help others.

2. Clara Barton was very shy and small, but she was also strong, could run fast, and ride a horse well. This helped make her popular with her students and with the soldiers during the Civil War. Why?

The Angel of the Battlefield
(1821–1912)

Clara Barton was so shy that her parents let her leave school and study at home, but later in life, she faced the bullets of the Confederate Army, argued with presidents, and became a popular public speaker. Clara Barton was born in North Oxford, Massachusetts, on December 25, 1821.

Clara was a small child, but she learned to ride horses well and to play ball, as well as to cook and sew. When she was only 11, her older brother David fell from a barn and almost died. For two years, she took care of him day and night. She was a born nurse.

At 17, Barton became a teacher in North Oxford. Later, she opened and taught in the first public school in Bordentown, New Jersey. She loved teaching, but she lost her voice one day and it remained weak. After 15 years in the classroom, she had to give up teaching. So she went to Washington, D.C., and got a job in the U.S. Patent Office.[1] She was the first woman to work there.

When Barton was in Washington, the Civil War between the North and the South began. At first, she worked as a volunteer nurse in a Washington hospital, but, in July 1862, she got permission to serve on the battlefields, where nurses were needed most, and where there were never enough bandages or food for the wounded. First, she collected food and medical supplies and stored them in her apartment. Then, when she heard of a battle near Washington, she loaded everything in a wagon and hurried to the battlefield.

She washed, bandaged, cooked for, and fed the wounded in open fields or in the houses, barns, and churches that were used as field hospitals. Hunger, pain, and blood were everywhere. She worked for days with very little sleep. Once a bullet put a big hole in her dress, but that didn't stop her. She wasn't afraid of bullets or death. The soldiers called her "The Angel of the Battlefield."

After the war, she fought another battle—the battle to get the President and the Senate to approve the Geneva Convention, an international treaty to protect the wounded and medical personnel in time of war.[2] In 1881, she established in the United States the Red Cross, an international organization that helps not only the victims of war, but of fires, floods, and hurricanes. She was the president of the American Red Cross from 1881 to 1904. She died in Glen Echo, Maryland, on April 12, 1912 at the age of 91.

[1] A **patent** is the exclusive right that the government gives to inventors to make and sell what they invent.

[2] President Chester Arthur signed the Geneva Convention and the Senate approved it in 1882.

I. Comprehension

Answer these questions about the story. Use your own ideas to answer the questions marked with a check ✔.

Paragraph 1

1. Why did Clara Barton leave school and study at home?

Paragraph 2

2. Name four things Clara learned to do as a child.
3. What happened to her brother David?

Paragraph 3

4. Why did Clara have to give up teaching?
✔ 5. Why does a teacher need a strong voice?

Paragraph 4

✔ 6. Why do you think it was difficult for Clara to get permission to go to the battlefields?
7. What did she collect and store in her apartment?
8. What did she do when she heard of a battle near Washington?

Paragraph 5

9. Name four things Clara did for the wounded.
10. What did the soldiers call her?

Paragraph 6

11. What was the aim of the Geneva Convention?
12. What does the Red Cross do?

II. Key Words

Before studying these words, reread the story and try to guess their meaning.

	Nouns		Verbs		Adjectives
bullet	battlefield	personnel	face (+n.)	store (+n.)	shy
voice	bandage (+v.)	organization	argue	load (+n.)	international
patent (+v.)	wagon	victim	sew	establish	
volunteer (+v.)	blood	flood (+v.)	wound (+n.)		**Other**
permission	angel	hurricane			as well as
			Irregular Pasts		(conj.)
			heard - hear		
			fed - feed		

III. Story Completion

Complete the story with these words.

bandaged	**voice**	**established**	**shy**	**loaded**
volunteer	**bullet**	**argued**	**wounded**	**permission**

Serving on the Battlefields

Clara Barton was born in Massachusetts on December 25, 1821.

She was so _____ that her parents let

her leave school and study at home, but later in life, she

_____ with Presidents and was a very good

public speaker.

At 17, she became a school teacher and taught for 15 years. But

one day she lost her _____ and had to give up

teaching. She got a job in the U.S. Patent Office in Washington,

D.C.

While Barton was in Washington, the Civil War began. At first,

she worked as a _____ in a Washington

hospital, but, in July 1862, she got _____ to serve on the battlefields. When she heard of a battle near Washington, she _____ food and medical supplies in a wagon and hurried to the battlefield.

Clara washed, _____ , cooked for, and fed the _____ in open fields or field hospitals. Once a _____ put a big hole in her dress, but that didn't stop her. She wasn't afraid.

After the Civil War, she worked hard to get the Geneva Convention approved, and in 1881, she _____ the Red Cross in the United States.

IV. Dialogs

Key Words

Nouns		Verbs		Other
courage	bravery	belong	appreciate	itself (pron.)
influence (+v.)	harm (+v.)	trouble (+n.)	stay out (of)	
		admire	involve	

Our Soldiers Are Dying

Clara Barton is helping the wounded in Washington, D.C., but she wants the Governor of Massachusetts to use his influence to get her permission to help them on the battlefield.

Complete the dialog with these words.

courage   **itself**   **influence**   **belong**   **troubles**

Governor: You're doing a great job helping the wounded.

Barton: But it's not enough.

Governor: What more can you do?

Barton: Go to the battlefield _____.

Governor: It won't be easy to get permission.

Barton: Why not? What's the problem?

Governor: They don't think that women _____
on battlefields.

Barton: Do you believe that?

Governor: Not in your case. You have a lot of _____.

Barton: Our soldiers are dying because we don't help them soon
enough.

Governor: That _____ me. I'll do what I can.

Barton: Thanks. Use all the _____ you have.

Protecting Our Wounded

It's after the Civil War, and Clara Barton is talking to President Rutherford B. Hayes, a Civil War hero. She wants him to sign the Geneva Convention. He's polite, but he doesn't want to. He sends her to the Secretary of State.

Complete the dialog with these words.

stay out	harm	bravery	involved	appreciates

Barton: Everyone admires your _____ in the Civil War.

Hayes: And the country _____ all you did.

Barton: War is terrible, but the Geneva Convention can help.

Hayes: Let me tell you what I think of it.

Barton: Please do.

Hayes: It's fine for Europe, but the United States doesn't need it.

Barton: But it'll protect our wounded and doctors in time of war.

Hayes: I plan to _____ of war.

Barton: Very good, but what _____ can the treaty do?

Hayes: A lot. Getting _____ in Europe is dangerous.

Barton: How will the treaty involve us in Europe?

Hayes: Talk to the Secretary of State. He'll explain it.

Barton: Thank you, Mr. President. I will.

Hayes: It was a pleasure to meet you, Miss Barton.

V. Sharing Ideas

Discuss these questions in pairs or small groups.

1. Clara Barton was very shy, especially as a child. But many people are shy. Do you think people are born shy, or do they become shy because of what happens to them?

2. Clara was a good teacher. Name some qualities a good teacher has.

3. Clara learned to ride a horse well and to cook well. How did this help her on the battlefield?

4. The armies in the the Civil War didn't have enough nurses. Who do you think helped the doctors?

5. Clara was able to work three or four days on the battlefield with very little sleep. Do you think many people could do that? Could you?

6. Name some qualities Clara showed as a nurse during the Civil War.

7. Today there are many women in the U.S. Army. Some say they shouldn't go into combat. Others say, "Why not?" What do you think? Explain your answer.

8. What do you know about the Red Cross? Does it continue to help the victims of war, fire, floods, and hurricanes? Did the Red Cross ever help you or anyone you know?

VI. Books You May Enjoy

1. Bains, Rae. *Clara Barton: Angel of the Battlefield.* Mahwah, New Jersey: Troll Associates, 1982. 48 pp. (Level 1)

2. Grant, Matthew G. *Clara Barton: Red Cross Pioneer.* Gallery of Great Americans Series. Mankato, Minnesota: Creative Education, 1974. 31 pp. (Level 1)

3. Sonneborn, Liz. *Clara Barton: Founder, American Red Cross.* Junior World Biographies. New York: Chelsea House Publishers, 1992. 79 pp. (Level 2)

4. Mann, Peggy. *Clara Barton, Battlefield Nurse.* New York: Coward-McCann, Inc., 1969. 124 pp. (Level 2)

*5. Hamilton, Leni. *Clara Barton: Founder, American Red Cross.* American Women of Achievement. New York: Chelsea House Publishers, 1988. 112 pp. (Level 3)

* Books with an asterisk are for teachers. They are too difficult for students using *Leaders of the Americas*.

5

African American Leaders

13 Harriet Tubman

Harriet Tubman

Important Events

1820, 1821 (?)	Harriet Ross is born in Maryland
1844	Marries John Tubman
1849	Escapes to freedom in Pennsylvania
1850–1860	Makes 19 trips to Maryland to lead slaves to freedom
1857	Buys house in Auburn, New York
1862–1863	Serves as nurse, scout, and spy for the Union Army
March 10, 1913	Dies in Auburn, New York at the age of 93

Preview

1. Imagine that you are a slave, that someone owns you. Your owner makes you work long hours picking cotton in the hot sun and beats you for little or no reason. You receive no pay, own nothing, have poor food, and terrible housing. You can't read or write and aren't allowed to learn. How do you feel?

2. Now imagine that you have the chance to escape. They will probably catch you, but maybe not. If they don't, you'll be free in the North. If they do, they'll kill you, or beat you and sell you. What are you going to do?

Harriet Tubman
(1820? – 1913)

Harriet Tubman was born in 1820 or 1821 on a plantation on the Eastern Shore of Maryland. No one knows the date of her birth because she was a slave, the property of a Mr. Edward Brodas. She was the youngest of 11 children, and she lived with her family in a one room shack with no windows and no beds. Her name was Harriet Ross and, in 1844, she married John Tubman.

Slavery was hell. When Harriet was only seven, she was hired out to a Miss Susan and made to clean her house and care for her baby. Miss Susan was cruel and frequently whipped Harriet. When she was ten, Harriet was hired out to a neighbor and had to work in his fields from dawn until dark. But her biggest fear was that one day she would be sold and led away in chains to the deep South, which often happened to slaves.

In 1849, at the age of 28, Tubman escaped from her owner and headed north on the Underground Railroad. This was not a real railroad, but a secret route to the North. On the "railroad" were houses where friendly whites and blacks hid and helped the runaway slaves. These houses were called "stations." Traveling by night and hiding by day, Tubman made her way to Pennsylvania. She was free at last. She felt she was in heaven.

Tubman went to Philadelphia and got a job as a maid and cook in a hotel. It was great to be free and to earn her own money, but she didn't know anyone in Philadelphia and was lonely. As she said later, "I was a stranger in a strange land."

One day she received word that they were selling her sister and her sister's two children. She traveled back to Maryland and guided her sister and her sister's family to Pennsylvania along the Underground Railroad. That was the beginning of her great mission in life—to help other slaves escape to the North. She returned to Maryland 19 times and led over 300

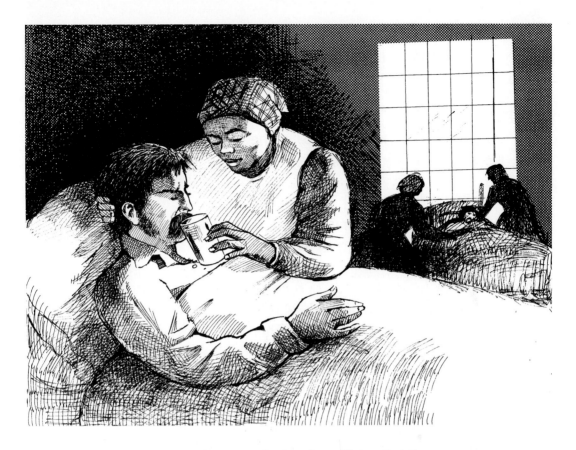

Harriet Tubman Caring for a Union Soldier

slaves to freedom. She was a "conductor" on the Underground Railroad, and she never lost a "passenger." She led so many out of slavery that people called her Moses.[1] The slave owners offered $40,000 in rewards for her capture, but she wasn't afraid. She put her complete trust in the Lord.

During the Civil War, she served in the Union Army in South Carolina as a nurse, a scout, and a spy. She cared for the sick and the wounded, but she also went behind enemy lines to spy on the Confederate Army. Once she led a raid that freed over 700 slaves and destroyed the supplies of the Confederate troops. After the war, she returned to her home in Auburn, New York, where she spent many years helping the poor and homeless. She died in Auburn on March 10, 1913 and was given a military funeral.

[1] **Moses** was a biblical leader who led the Jewish people from a life of slavery in Egypt to freedom.

I. Comprehension

Answer these questions about the story. Use your own ideas to answer the questions marked with a check ✔.

Paragraph 1

✔ 1. Why didn't they keep records of the births of slaves?

2. Describe the "house" that Harriet Tubman lived in.

Paragraph 2

3. What did Harriet Tubman have to do for Miss Susan?

4. What was Harriet's biggest fear?

Paragraph 3

5. What was the Underground Railroad?

6. How did Harriet Tubman feel when she entered Pennsylvania as a free person?

Paragraph 4

7. What was Harriet Tubman's first job?

8. Why was she lonely?

Paragraph 5

9. What was Harriet Tubman's great mission in life?

10. How many times did she return to Maryland? How many slaves did she lead to freedom?

Paragraph 6

11. What did Harriet Tubman do in the Union Army?

✔ 12. Why do you think she made a good spy?

II. Key Words

Before studying these words, reread the story and try to guess their meaning.

Nouns			Verbs	Irregular Pasts	Adjectives
shore	chains	capture (+v.)	hire out	hid - hide	eastern
property	station (+v.)	trust (+v.)	whip (+n.)	led - lead	cruel
shack	maid	scout (+v.)	head (+n.)		deep
hell	stranger	spy (+v.)	earn		underground
heaven	conductor	raid (+v.)	guide (+n.)		runaway (+n.)
dawn	passenger	funeral			strange
	reward (+v.)				lonely
					homeless (+n.)

III. Story Completion

Complete the story with these words.

rewards	headed	property	lonely	hiding
chains	led	spy	whipped	maid

Escape to the North

Harriet Tubman was a slave, the _____ of a

Mr. Edward Brodas. When she was only seven, she was hired out to

a Miss Susan, who was cruel and frequently _____

her. But her biggest fear was that she would be sold and led away

in _____ to the deep South.

When she was 28, Tubman escaped from her owner and

_____ north on the Underground Railroad.

Traveling by night and _____ by day, she

made her way to Pennsylvania. She was free at last.

Tubman went to Philadelphia, where she worked as a

_____ and cook in a hotel, but she didn't

know anyone in Philadelphia and she was _____.

Tubman returned to Maryland 19 times and _____
more than 300 slaves to freedom. That was why the slave owners
offered $40,000 in _____ for her capture.

During the Civil War, Tubman served in the Union Army as a
nurse, scout, and a _____. After the war, she
returned to her home in Auburn, New York, where she helped the
poor and homeless.

IV. Dialogs

Key Words

Nouns		Verbs		Adjectives
fool (+v.)	cane	freeze (+n.)	rescue (+n.)	satisfied
sign (+v.)	pistol	report (+n.)	recognize	clever

I Want to Be Free

In 1844, Harriet Ross married John Tubman, a free African American. In 1849, when Harriet decided to escape and go north, she wanted her husband to go with her, but he wouldn't.

Complete the dialog with these words.

freeze   **report**   **fool**   **satisfied**   **signs**

Harriet: I'm planning to escape. Come with me!

John: Don't be a _____. You'll never make it.

Harriet: I have to try. I want to be free.

John: They'll catch you and whip you to death.

Harriet: The Lord will be with me. I'm not afraid.

John: But you don't know the way and you can't read

_____.

Harriet: I can read the sky. I'll follow the North Star.

John: Why risk so much to live and _____ in the North?

Harriet: It's a small price to pay for freedom.

John: Well, I'm _____ here. This is my home.

Harriet: I want you to come with me, John. I love you.

John: I won't. And if you try to escape, I'll _____ you.

Harriet: I can't believe that. How could you?

John: Get those crazy ideas out of your head, and I won't have to.

Harriet: Never! I shall be free, or I shall die!

To Maryland Again

William Still, an African American businessman in Philadelphia, was active in helping runaway slaves and was a good friend of Harriet Tubman. It's 1857, and he's talking to Harriet about her trip to Maryland to rescue her parents.

Complete the dialog with these words.

disguises   cane   recognize   trust   clever

William: Why are you going to Maryland again?

Harriet: To rescue my parents.

William: Aren't you afraid someone will _____ you?

Harriet: Yes, that's why I use _____.

William: Like what?

Harriet: Sometimes I dress as a man.

William: That's _____.

Harriet: And sometimes I walk with a _____ like an old lady.

William: And what's that you've got?

Harriet: A pistol.

William: I thought you put your _____ in the Lord.

Harriet: I do, but He also wants us to protect ourselves.

William: You're right. Be careful and good luck!

V. Sharing Ideas

Discuss these questions in pairs or small groups.

1. To escape, Harriet Tubman had to break many laws. To help the runaway slaves, the people on the Underground Railroad had to break the law. When is it right to break the law?

2. Why do you think that Harriet Tubman and many slaves were so religious?

3. How did slavery hurt slaves physically?

4. How did it hurt them psychologically?

5. Harriet Tubman was intelligent, but she couldn't read or write because slaves weren't allowed to learn those skills. Why were slave owners afraid to let slaves learn to read and write?

6. Slaves were very happy to be free, but their new lives were also very difficult. Why?

7. Can you give examples from recent times of people escaping from their countries because they wanted to be free?

8. What did Clara Barton and Harriet Tubman have in common?

VI. Books You May Enjoy

1. Smith, Kathie Billingslea. *Harriet Tubman*. The Great American Series. New York: Simon and Schuster, Inc., 1988. 23 pp. (Level 1)

2. Polcovar, Jane. *What Was It Like? Harriet Tubman*. What Was It Like? Series. Stamford, Connecticut: Longmeadow Press, 1988. 48 pp. (Level 2)

3. Stein, R. Conrad. *The Story of the Underground Railroad*. Cornerstones of Freedom. Chicago: Childrens Press, 1981. 31 pp. (Level 2)

*4. Carlson, Judy. *Harriet Tubman: Call to Freedom*. The Great Lives Series. New York: Fawcett Columbine, 1989. 116 pp. (Level 3)

* Books with an asterisk are for teachers. They are too difficult for students using *Leaders of the Americas*.

14 Booker T. Washington

Booker T. Washington Addressing a Large Crowd

<table>
<tr><td colspan="2" align="center">Important Events</td></tr>
<tr><td align="right">April 5, 1856</td><td>Booker T. Washington is born near Hale's Ford, Virginia</td></tr>
<tr><td align="right">1865</td><td>Moves with his family to Malden, West Virginia</td></tr>
<tr><td align="right">1872–1875</td><td>Attends Hampton Institute in Hampton, Virginia</td></tr>
<tr><td align="right">July 4, 1881</td><td>Opens Tuskegee Institute in Tuskegee, Alabama</td></tr>
<tr><td align="right">1895</td><td>Gives speech at Exposition in Atlanta, Georgia</td></tr>
<tr><td align="right">1901</td><td>Publishes his autobiography, Up From Slavery</td></tr>
<tr><td align="right">November 10, 1915</td><td>Dies in Tuskegee, Alabama at the age of 59</td></tr>
</table>

Preview

1. Booker T. Washington was born a slave. He couldn't read or write until he started night school when he was nine. But he studied hard, did well in school, and became a great African American educator and leader. He's a good example of how much hard work and education can do for a person.

2. Booker T. Washington got along well with white leaders and was careful to please them, and they helped him to make Tuskegee Institute an excellent school. But his desire to please and need for white support made it difficult for him to protest when African Americans were not given their civil rights.

Booker T. Washington
(1856–1915)

Booker T. Washington was born in Virginia on April 5, 1856. He was a slave until the Civil War ended in 1865. His mother, Jane Ferguson, cried for joy when she heard that all Negroes[1] were free at last. After she was free, she took Booker and her other two children to Malden, West Virginia to join her husband (Booker's stepfather).

Although Booker was only nine, he had to go to work to help support the family. First, he worked at a salt furnace, shoveling salt into big barrels. Later, he got a job in a coal mine. Work in the mines was extremely difficult, dirty, and dangerous, and Booker hated it. He was eager to learn to read and write, so he worked all day and went to school at night. One day at work, he heard two miners talking about a boarding school for Negroes in Hampton, Virginia. He decided that he would go to that school.

When Washington was 16, he set out for Hampton Institute. The trip was 500 miles, and by the time he got to Richmond, Virginia, he didn't have any money left for food or lodging, so he slept under a bridge. The next day he got a job unloading a ship to make some money to eat and to continue his trip. He arrived at Hampton Institute tired, dirty, and hungry. He didn't look like a student and had only 50 cents in his pocket.

Hampton Institute seemed like the promised land to Washington, but the principal of Hampton hesitated to accept him because of his appearance. Then the principal asked him to sweep a room. This was his "entrance exam." He did such a good job that she accepted him, and he was thrilled. Washington became the school janitor to pay for his room and board. After he graduated from Hampton Institute, he taught for a few years in Malden before going back to Hampton to teach. While at Hampton, he got his big opportunity.

He was only 25, but the head of Hampton Institute recommended that Washington be put in charge of a new school for Negroes in Tuskegee,

Booker T. Washington in His Office at Tuskegee

Alabama. When Washington arrived in Tuskegee, he discovered that his school had no buildings, books, or supplies. But that didn't discourage him for long. On July 4, 1881, ten days after his arrival, he opened up Tuskegee Institute in an old church building. Washington devoted the rest of his life to improving and expanding Tuskegee. The purpose of the school was to train teachers, carpenters, plumbers, bricklayers, and farmers. Booker believed strongly in the dignity of manual labor.

Washington was a great public speaker and, in September 1895, he gave a speech at the Cotton States and International Exposition in Atlanta. This speech made him famous. In it he said, "In all things that are purely social, we can be as separate as the fingers, yet one as the hand in all things essential to mutual progress." Booker's emphasis was always on education, self-help, and economic progress. He did not push hard for civil rights. He felt that education and economic improvement would lead to equality and full civil rights for his people.

At the beginning of November 1915, Washington was in New York City giving speeches, and raising money for Tuskegee. He fell sick and, when his condition got worse, it was apparent that he was going to die. He asked to be taken back to Tuskegee. "I was born in the South, and I expect to die and be buried in the South." He arrived at Tuskegee on the afternoon of November 12th and died on the 13th at 4:45 AM. The Negro community had lost a great educator and leader.

[1] Since Washington called African Americans *Negroes*, this story and the dialogs in this chapter will do the same. African American is a more modern expression.

I. Comprehension

Answer these questions about the story. Use your own ideas to answer the questions marked with a check ✔.

Paragraph 1

1. What did Booker T. Washington's mother do when she heard that all Negroes were free?

Paragraph 2

2. What was Booker T. Washington's first job?
3. How do we know that he was eager to read and write?

Paragraph 3

4. Where did Washington sleep in Richmond, Virginia?
5. How did he get money to eat and continue his trip?

Paragraph 4

6. What was Washington's "entrance exam" to Hampton Institute?
✔ 7. What do you think the principal was trying to test by this exam?

Paragraph 5

✔ 8. Washington opened Tuskegee Institute in ten days despite many difficulties. What does that tell us about him?
9. What was the aim of Tuskegee?

Paragraph 6

10. What did Washington emphasize for his people?
11. What didn't he push hard?

Paragraph 7

12. What was Washington doing when he fell sick in New York City?

II. Key Words

Before studying these words, reread the story and try to guess their meaning.

Nouns		Verbs		Adjectives	
stepfather	janitor	shovel (+n.)	recommend	eager (to)	worse
furnace	board	unload	discourage	essential	apparent
barrel	exposition	promise (+n.)	devote	mutual	
mine	progress (+v.)	hesitate	expand		
lodging	self-help	thrill (+n.)		**Other**	
appearance	condition	**Irregular Past**		at last (idiom)	
boarding school		slept - sleep		extremely (adv.)	

III. Story Completion

Complete the story with these words.

lodging   manual   recommended   eager   thrilled
shoveling   unloading   progress   hesitated   expanding

Education and Self-Help

When Booker T. Washington was nine, he got his first job. He

worked at a salt furnace, _____ salt into big

barrels. Later, he worked in a coal mine. He was _____

to learn to read, so he went to school at night.

When Washington was 16, he set out for Hampton Institute. By

the time he got to Richmond, Virginia, he didn't have any money

left for food or _____. To make some money,

he got a job _____ a ship.

The principal of Hampton Institute _____

to accept Washington because of his appearance. After he did

a great job sweeping a room, she accepted him; he was

_____.

A few years after Washington's graduation from Hampton Institute, the head of Hampton _____ that Washington be put in charge of a new school in Tuskegee. He devoted the rest of his life to improving and _____ Tuskegee.

Washington emphasized the importance of education, self-help, and economic _____ , and he believed strongly in the dignity of _____ labor.

IV. Dialogs

Key Words

Nouns		Verbs		Adjectives
brick	approach (+v.)	construct	insist	theoretical
pride	optimism	admire	differ	negative
		protest (+n.)	exaggerate	
		cooperate	complain	

Hard Work and Optimism

Booker T. Washington had many friends and a lot of influence in high places. President Theodore Roosevelt was one of his friends and invited him to dinner at the White House.

Complete the dialog with these words.

admire   **construct**   **honor**   **self-help**   **bricks**

T. Roosevelt: Welcome to the White House, Mr. Washington!

Washington: Thank you, Mr. President. It's a great _____ to be here.

T. Roosevelt: How's everything at Tuskegee?

Washington: Fine. We're putting up new buildings all the time.

T. Roosevelt: That must be expensive.

Washington: It is, but we make our own _____.

T. Roosevelt: That's wonderful!

Washington: And the students _____ the buildings themselves.

T. Roosevelt: That must save a lot of money.

Washington: It does, but it's also a matter of pride and

_____.

T. Roosevelt: I _____ your hard work and optimism.

Washington: Thank you, Mr. President. I do my best.

Education First

Mr. W.E.B. Du Bois, also a Negro leader, criticized Mr. Washington for not protesting that Negroes weren't being given their rights, for example, the right to vote. A reporter asks Washington what he thinks of Du Bois.

Complete the dialog with these words.

approach   exaggerates   cooperate   theoretical   insist

Reporter: What do you think of Mr. Du Bois?

Washington: Well, we're certainly different.

Reporter: In what way?

Washington: He likes to protest.

Reporter: And you?

Washington: I like to _____. Negroes and whites have to work together.

Reporter: But are whites willing to cooperate?

Washington: Many of them are.

Reporter: Why don't you _____ more on the rights of Negroes?

Washington: My _____ is to put education first.

Reporter: How else do you differ from Mr. Du Bois?

Washington: I'm very practical.

Reporter: Are you saying he's too _____?

Washington: Yes, I am. And too negative.

Reporter: What do you mean?

Washington: He _____ our problems and complains too much.

Reporter: But don't you have many problems?

Washington: Yes, but we also have a lot of opportunities and a bright future.

V. Sharing Ideas

Discuss these questions in pairs or small groups.

1. Booker T. Washington worked at a salt furnace when he was only nine. Is it possible for a nine year old to work in a factory today? Why not?

2. Washington almost didn't get into Hampton Institute because of his appearance. Do people often judge others by their appearances? Is that right? Explain your answer.

3. Washington was willing to accept segregation in "all things that are purely social" in order to emphasize education and economic progress. What do you think of this approach? Explain your answer.

4. Washington pointed out that one third of the South was Negro and that the progress of the South depended on the progress of the Negro. Do you think that the progress of most U.S. cities today depends on the progress of African Americans? Explain your answer.

5. Washington believed strongly in the dignity of physical labor, in the importance of training plumbers, electricians, carpenters, bricklayers, etc. How important are these jobs to the economy? Do they pay well?

6. One of the aims of Tuskegee was to train Negro teachers. Why were there so few Negro teachers in the South after the Civil War?

Is it important that a school with a large number of African American students have a number of African American teachers? Explain your answer.

7. The Reverend Jessie Jackson, a well-known African American leader, is quick to protest, but he also emphasizes self-help. Do you think he's trying to combine the best of Washington and Du Bois? Explain your answer.

8. Reread the life of Harriet Tubman (pages 118–119). How were the lives of Tubman and Washington similar? How were they different?

VI. Books You May Enjoy

1. Paterson, Lillie G. *Booker T. Washington*. Discovery Book. Champaign, Illinois: Garrard Publishing Company, 1962. 80 pp. (Level 1)

2. Wise, William. *Booker T. Washington*. See and Read Biography. New York: G.P. Putnam's Sons, 1968. 64 pp. (Level 1)

*3. Washington, Booker T. *Up From Slavery*. New York: Doubleday, Page & Co., 1901; Penguin Books USA Inc., 1986. 332 pp. (Level 3)

*4. Schroeder, Alan. *Booker T. Washington: Educator and Racial Spokesman*. Black Americans of Achievement. New York: Chelsea House Publishers, 1992. 143 pp. (Level 3)

* Books with an asterisk are for teachers. They are too difficult for students using *Leaders of the Americas*.

6

Latin Leaders

15 Simón Bolívar

Simón Bolívar

Important Events

June 24, 1783	Simón Bolívar is born in Caracas, Venezuela
May 26, 1802	Marries María Teresa Rodríguez in Madrid
January 22, 1803	María Teresa dies in Caracas
August 15, 1804	Bolívar visits Rome and vows to free Venezuela
August 17, 1819	Wins major victory at Boyacá, Colombia
December 17, 1819	Venezuela, Colombia, and Ecuador become one country
December 17, 1830	Bolívar dies in Santa Marta, Colombia

Preview

1. Simón Bolívar is the George Washington of Venezuela, Colombia, Ecuador, Peru, and Bolivia. He was a great general and freed these five South American countries from the rule of Spain. Like Washington, he lost many battles before he won the war and independence for his countries. Did you know anything about the life of Simón Bolívar before reading this paragraph? What did you know?

2. When Venezuela, Colombia, and Ecuador won independence, they became one country with Bolívar as their President. But they soon separated. Today these countries are working together more closely. Do you think they will ever become one country again? Explain your answer.

Simón Bolívar
(1783 – 1830)

Simón Bolívar was born of wealthy parents in Caracas, Venezuela on June 24, 1783. His father died when he was three, and his mother when he was nine. He lived with his grandfather for two years, and when his grandfather died, Bolívar went to live with his uncle. His uncle hired a tutor, Simón Rodríguez, who had a great influence on Bolívar's life. He taught him to love books and, above all, to love freedom.

When Bolívar was 16, he went to Spain to finish his education. He lived there for three years and fell in love with María Teresa Rodríguez. They were married on May 26, 1802 and went to Venezuela to live. María died of yellow fever on January 22, 1803, less than eight months after their marriage. It was the saddest day of Bolívar's life. He was only 19, but he decided never to marry again.

Bolívar turned his attention to politics. Although he loved Spain, he hated Spain's rule of Venezuela and South America. When he was in Rome in 1804, he made a vow, a special promise to God, not to rest until he freed Venezuela from the tyranny of Spain. He joined the others who were fighting for the independence of Venezuela and New Granada (modern Colombia) and became a general.

Bolívar lost many battles and had to flee from Venezuela more than once, but he never quit. He came back and, on August 17, 1819, won a major victory at Boyacá, a small town just outside of Bogotá, Colombia. Bolívar and his army had more battles to fight, but Boyacá was the turning point in their struggle for independence.

On December 17, 1819, Venezuela, New Granada, and Ecuador became one country, Gran Colombia. This was Bolívar's dream! He also freed Peru and Bolivia with the help of José Antonio de Sucre, a great general and a close friend. Bolívar became the President of the five

The Five Countries Liberated by Bolívar

countries he had freed, and he wrote a constitution for Bolivia, a country named for him. He had the personal glory he wanted, but his happiness didn't last long. Nationalism soon destroyed the unity of Gran Colombia; and Venezuela, Colombia, and Ecuador became separate countries.

Some men actually tried to kill Bolívar, and he was lucky to escape with the help of his good friend Manuela Saenz. His enemies were no longer from Spain, but from the countries he loved and liberated. He had won the war, but he seemed to be losing the peace. He wasn't well and he was discouraged. No one was listening to him. He resigned from the Presidency and considered living in Europe, but stayed in Colombia. He died on December 17, 1830, in Santa Marta, Colombia; poor, unhappy, and unpopular. But soon after his death, he was recognized as South America's greatest leader and general, and honored as the Great Liberator.

I. Comprehension

Answer these questions about the story. Use your own ideas to answer the questions marked with a check ✔.

Paragraph 1

1. Where was Simón Bolívar born?
2. What, above all, did his tutor Simón Rodríguez teach him?

Paragraph 2

3. What happened to Bolívar when he went to Spain to study?
4. What happened to María Teresa less than eight months after her marriage?

Paragraph 3

✔ 5. Why do you think Bolívar hated the rule of Spain in Venezuela and South America?
6. What vow, what promise to God, did he make in Rome?

Paragraph 4

7. Why did Bolívar have to flee from Venezuela more than once?
8. What victory was the turning point of the struggle for independence?

Paragraph 5

9. Bolívar freed and become the President of what five countries?
10. Who helped him free Peru and Bolivia?
11. What destroyed the unity of Gran Colombia?

Paragraph 6

✔ 12. When they were at war with Spain, it was easier for the other political leaders in Colombia and Venezuela to support Bolívar than after the war. Why?

II. Key Words

Before studying these words, reread the story and try to guess their meaning.

Nouns	Verbs	Adjectives
influence (+v.)	hate (+n.)	wealthy
yellow fever	flee	major
rule (+v.)	destroy	personal
vow (+v.)	liberate	
tyranny	discourage	**Other**
struggle (+v.)		above all (idiom)
glory	**Irregular Past**	less than (conj.)
nationalism	quit - quit	although (conj.)
liberator		just (adv., +adj.)
		actually (adv.)

III. Story Completion

Complete the story with these words.

liberated	tyranny	quit	above all	destroyed
major	discouraged	struggle	flee	although

The Great Liberator

Simón Bolívar was born in Caracas, Venezuela, on June 24, 1783. Simón Rodríguez, his tutor, taught him to love books and, _____ , to love freedom.

_____ Bolívar liked Spain, he hated its rule of Venezuela and South America. He made a vow not to rest until he freed Venezuela from the _____ of Spain.

Bolívar lost many battles and had to _____ from Venezuela more than once, but he never _____.

In August 1819, he won a _____ victory

at Boyacá, Colombia. This victory was the turning point in the

_____ for independence.

In December 1819, Venezuela, New Granada, and Ecuador became one country, Gran Colombia. But nationalism soon _____ its unity.

Some men tried to kill Bolívar. His enemies were no longer from Spain, but from the countries he loved and _____.
He wasn't well and was _____. No one was listening to him. So he resigned from the Presidency. He died on December 17, 1830.

IV. Dialogs

Key Words

Nouns		Verbs		Adjective	Other
colonel	pistol	march (+n.)	warn	brave	what's the matter
palace	sword	unite	shout (+n.)		(idiom)
death	council room				quickly (adv.)

We'll March Over the Andes

Bolívar is discussing with one of his colonels his plan to cross the Andes and surprise the Spanish army in New Granada (Colombia).

Complete the dialog with these words.

brave   attack   dream   across   unite

Bolívar: I'm going to _____ the Spanish
Army in New Granada.

Colonel: But we're in Venezuela. How are you going to get there?

Bolívar: We'll march _____ the Andes.

Colonel: That's impossible!

Bolívar: We can do it. Our men are _____.

Colonel: Does that mean you plan to free New Granada first?

Bolívar: Yes, and then go back and free Venezuela.

Colonel: Do you want to make Venezuela and New Granada one country?

Bolívar: Exactly. I plan to _____ them.

Colonel: That's a great idea, but it won't work.

Bolívar: Maybe not, but I have to try. It's my _____.

Death to Bolívar!

Manuela Saenz, a close friend of Bolívar, is warning him that a group of men is at the door of the Presidential palace shouting, "Death to Bolívar!"

Complete the dialog with these words.

quickly	matter	sword	still	shouting

Manuela: Wake up! Wake up!

Bolívar: What's the _____?

Manuela: There are some men at the door of the palace.

Bolívar: What do they want?

Manuela: To kill you!

Bolívar: Are you sure?

Manuela: Yes, yes! They're _____, "Death to Bolívar!"

Bolívar: I have my pistol and _____.

Manuela: There are too many of them to fight.

Bolívar: You're right, but I _____ have time to escape.

Manuela: Go _____! I'll say you're in the council room.

Bolívar: Good. I'll go out the back window.

V. Sharing Ideas

Discuss these questions in pairs or small groups.

1. When Simón Bolívar was 16, he went to Spain to finish his education. Why do you think that many sons of the rich went from South America to Spain to finish their education?

2. When Bolívar's wife died, he was only 19 and had no children. He decided not to marry again out of love for his wife. What do you think of this decision?

3. What are some of the good qualities we see in Bolívar in his long fight for independence?

4. Do you think it was realistic for Bolívar to become the President of five countries? Explain your answer.

5. Reread the life of Washington, and then compare Bolívar and Washington. Who was probably the greater military leader? Who had more success as a leader in peace time?

6. Compare the War of Independence of the English colonies and that of the Spanish colonies under Bolívar.

7. What do you know about Venezuela? Where is it located? What are its main cities? What is its capital? How large is it? What is its population? Describe its climate. Describe its economy. What kind of government does it have? Have the students work in small groups. Each group should give a brief report answering two or three of the questions. One group should include a map of Venezuela.

8. Ask the same questions about Colombia, Ecuador, Peru, and Bolivia. Have the students work in groups. Each group should give a brief report answering two or three of the questions. One group should include a map.

VI. Books You May Enjoy

1. Gleiter, Jan, and Kathleen Thompson. *Simón Bolívar*. Hispanic Stories. Austin, Texas: Steck-Vaughn, 1991. 32 pp. (Level 1)

2. Syme, Ronald. *Bolívar the Liberator*. New York: William Morrow and Company, 1968. 192 pp. (Level 2)

*3. Bailey, Bernadine. *Famous Latin-American Liberators*. New York: Dodd, Mead & Company, 1960. 158 pp. (Level 3)

* Books with an asterisk are for teachers. They are too difficult for students using *Leaders of the Americas.*

16 Benito Juárez

Benito Juárez

Important Events

March 21, 1806	Benito Juárez is born in San Pablo Guelatao, Mexico
1831	Receives his law degree
July 31, 1843	Marries Margarita Maza
1848	Is elected Governor of the state of Oaxaca
June 11, 1861	Is elected President of Mexico
July 18, 1867	Returns to Mexico City after the French leave
July 18, 1872	Dies of a heart attack in Mexico City

Preview

1. Young Benito Juárez had no money, no influence, and was a Native Mexican, a Zapotec Indian. In the society of his day, he was considered a nobody, but he became the President of Mexico. Why was a good education so important to him?

2. When Juárez became the Governor of the state of Oaxaca, he built many public schools and hospitals to help the poor. Why do you think he did so much for the poor?

Benito Juárez
(1806–1872)

Benito Juárez was born in Mexico in the mountain village of San Pablo Guelatao in the state of Oaxaca on March 21, 1806. Both of his parents were Zapotec Indians. His mother and father died when he was three, and he went to live with his uncle. What he wanted most as a child was a good education, but there were no schools in his village. At the age of 12, he ran away to the city of Oaxaca, where his sister was a cook and where there were schools. He found work and a place to live with Antonio Salanueva, a bookbinder who treated him like a son and sent him to school.

After studying for the priesthood for six years, Juárez left the seminary and studied physics and law at the Oaxaca Institute of Arts and Sciences. In 1831, he received a law degree and started practicing law. In 1843, he married Margarita Maza, the youngest daughter of the Maza family. She was only 17 and he was 37. Despite the big difference in their ages, they had a very happy marriage.

In 1848, Juárez was elected Governor of the state of Oaxaca. This was a great honor and a big responsibility. He built hospitals, roads, and over 200 new schools. He did everything he could to help the poor, and he was very honest.

An enemy of Juárez, Santa Ana, became the dictator of Mexico in 1853. He put Juárez in jail and then sent him into exile. Juárez lived in New Orleans for two years before returning to Mexico to help defeat Santa Ana. Juárez was named Minister of Justice in the new government and was responsible for passing *La Ley Juárez*, the Juárez Law. This law eliminated special courts for the clergy and the military. It made all Mexicans equal before the law.

Juárez was elected President of Mexico in 1861. When he stopped payment of foreign debts, England, France, and Spain sent troops to Mexico. The English and Spanish soon left, but not the French. On May 5, 1862,[1] the Mexican Army defeated a large French force at Puebla, but a year later the French captured Mexico City. They made Archduke Maximilian of Austria the Emperor of Mexico. Juárez refused to accept a foreign ruler, and for three years he fought the French from northern

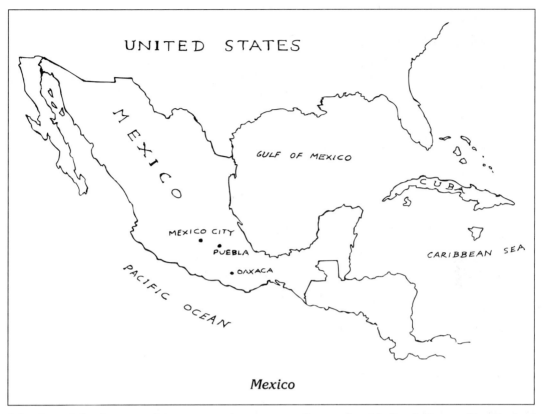

Mexico

Mexico. Mexican resistance and pressure from the United States finally led the French to withdraw their troops in 1867. Juárez returned to Mexico City in triumph and restored the Mexican government.

Juárez was reelected President in 1867 and again in 1871. On July 19, 1872, he died of a massive heart attack at the age of 66. Mexico mourned the loss of a President who had devoted his life to helping the poor, to improving education and the law, and to obtaining equality for all. Known for his honesty and love of country, he was Mexico's greatest President and won respect for all Native Mexicans.

1 May 5th, *el cinco de mayo*, is a national holiday in Mexico.

I. Comprehension

Answer these questions about the story. Use your own ideas to answer the questions marked with a check ✔.

Paragraph 1

1. What did Benito Juárez do at the age of 12?
2. Why did he go to the city of Oaxaca? Give two reasons.

Paragraph 2

3. What did Juárez receive in 1831?

✔ 4. Juárez wasn't handsome or rich, and he was 20 years older than Margarita Maza. Why do you think she was attracted to him?

Paragraph 3

5. To what position was Juárez elected in 1848?
6. Name three things he built in Oaxaca.

Paragraph 4

7. What did Santa Ana do to Juárez?
8. What did *La Ley Juárez*, the Juárez Law, eliminate?

✔ 9. Juárez fought to make all Mexicans equal before the law. Why do you think this was so important to him?

Paragraph 5

10. Why did England, France, and Spain send troops to Mexico?
11. Why did the French withdraw their troops in 1867?

Paragraph 6

12. To what had Juárez devoted his life? Name three things.

II. Key Words

Before studying these words, reread the story and try to guess their meaning.

Nouns		Verbs	Adjectives
village	exile (+v.)	pass (+n.)	responsible
bookbinder	debt	eliminate	foreign
priesthood	troops	refuse	massive
seminary	force (+v.)	withdraw	
clergy	emperor		**Other**
degree	resistance	**Irregular Past**	both (pron., adj.)
responsibility	pressure (+v.)	sent - send	desite (prep.)
dictator	triumph (+v.)		over (prep., adv., adj.)
jail (+v.)			

III. Story Completion

Complete the story with these words.

pressure	eliminated	village	responsibility	withdraw
despite	massive	exile	sent	foreign

President of Mexico

Benito Juárez was born in Mexico in a mountain _____ in the state of Oaxaca on March 21, 1806. He found work and a place to live with Antonio Salanueva who treated him like a son and _____ him to school.

In 1843, Juárez married Margarita Maza _____ the big difference in their ages. He was 37; she was 17. In 1848, he was elected Governor of Oaxaca, a big honor and _____.

Santa Ana, the dictator of Mexico, put Juárez in jail and sent him into _____ in 1853. When Juárez returned to Mexico, he joined the new government and was responsible for passing the Juárez Law. This law _____ special courts for the clergy and the military.

Juárez was elected President of Mexico in 1861. In 1863, the French captured Mexico City and made Maximilian of Austria the Emperor of Mexico, but Juárez refused to accept a _____ ruler. Mexican resistance and _____ from the United States led the French to _____ their troops in 1867.

Juárez was reelected President in 1867 and again in 1871, but he died of a _____ heart attack on July 19, 1872.

IV. Dialogs

Key Words

Nouns	Verbs		Adjectives
interest (+v.)	propose	near (+adj., adv., prep.)	enough (+adv., pron.)
traitor	matter (+n.)	head (+n.)	
coach	share	join	**Other**
	go ahead		whoa (interjection)
			crazy about (idiom)

Caring and Very Intelligent

Seventeen-year-old Margarita Maza is asking her father for permission to marry Benito Juárez. Benito is 37.

Complete the dialog with these words.

understanding   enough   proposed   of course   matter

Margarita: Dad, I want to marry Benito Juárez.

Mr. Maza: Whoa! Did you say marry? Did you say Benito Juárez?

Margarita: Yes, I'm crazy about him! And last night he

_____ to me.

Mr. Maza: But you're only 17!

Margarita: A lot of girls marry at 17.

Mr. Maza: But Benito's 37. He's old _____ to be your father.

Margarita: Age doesn't _____. We're in love.

Mr. Maza: There's a lot more to marriage than love.

Margarita: What do you mean?

Mr. Maza: There has to be _____ and common interests.

Margarita: _____ , Dad, but we share many interests, and he understands me.

Mr. Maza: Okay. Go ahead. I know he's caring and very intelligent.

Margarita: Thanks, Dad! You're wonderful!

No Ifs, Ands, or Buts!

Benito Juárez is talking to his military commander, General Jesús Ortega. A large French Army is advancing on Mexico City.

Complete the dialog with these words.

join	beat	traitor	head	nearing

Ortega: French troops are _____ Mexico City.

Juárez: Well, we _____ them last May at Puebla.

Ortega: True, but we can't do it this time.

Juárez: Then I'll leave the capital and _____ north.

Ortega: Maximilian wants you to _____ his government.

Juárez: Never! Never! I'm not a _____!

Ortega: Of course not, but . . .

Juárez: No ifs, ands, or buts about it! Mexico must be for Mexicans.

Ortega: Okay. Your coach is ready. We have to hurry.

Juárez: We'll go to Monterrey.

Ortega: And what about your wife and children?

Juárez: If necessary, I'll send them to the United States.

V. Sharing Ideas

Discuss these questions in pairs or small groups.

1. Margarita Maza was only 17 when she married Benito Juárez. Today most women marry at a later age. Why?

2. Benito Juárez was 20 years older than his wife. Do you think that's usually too great a difference for a couple to marry? Or do you believe that age doesn't matter if a couple is in love?

3. Five of Margarita and Benito Juárez's 12 children died when they were young. Many more young children died in those days than today. Why?

4. Why do you think Juárez met with prejudice when he lived in New Orleans from 1853 to 1855?

5. When France sent troops to Mexico in 1861 and kept them there, the United States was unhappy, but didn't do much. What was happening in the United States that kept it from acting?

6. Both of Juárez's parents were Zapotec Indians. Do you think his life helped Mexico to accept Native Mexicans as equals? Explain your answer.

7. Reread the story of Abraham Lincoln (pages 90–91), and compare the lives of Juárez and Lincoln. How were they alike? How were they different?

8. What do you know about Mexico? Where is it located? What are its main cities? What is its capital? How large is it? What is its population? Describe its climate. Describe its economy. What kind of government does it have? Have the students work in small groups. Each group should give a brief report answering two or three of the questions. One group should include a map of Mexico.

VI. Books You May Enjoy

1. Bains, Rae. *Benito Juárez: Hero of Modern Mexico*. Mahwah, New Jersey: Troll Associates, 1993. 48 pp. (Level 1)

2. Gleiter, Jan. *Benito Juárez*. Hispanic Stories. Austin, Texas: Steck-Vaughn, 1990. 32 pp. (Level 1)

*3. Bailey, Bernadine. *Famous Latin-American Liberators*. New York: Dodd, Mead & Company, 1960. 158 pp. (Level 3)

* Books with an asterisk are for teachers. They are too difficult for students using *Leaders of the Americas*.

17 José Martí

José Martí

Important Events

January 28, 1853	José Martí is born in Havana, Cuba
1868–1878	Ten Years' War between Spain and Cuba
March 4, 1870	Martí is sentenced to prison for writing a letter
June 30, 1874	Receives a law degree from the University of Zaragoza
December 20, 1877	Marries Carmen Zayas Bazán in Mexico City
November 22, 1878	Their son José is born in Havana
1880–1895	Lives in New York, organizing an invasion of Cuba
May 27, 1895	Is killed in battle at Dos Ríos, Cuba

Preview

1. José Martí, a Cuban writer and leader, lived in exile in New York City for 15 years, from 1880–1895. At that time, many Cubans lived in New York and Florida because they were sent into exile, or didn't like the Spanish rule in Cuba. Why are many Cubans living in New York and Florida today?

2. José Martí lived and died for one thing, a free and independent Cuba. What is the political situation in Cuba today? Is Fidel Castro still in power? Are the Cuban people free?

José Martí
(1853–1895)

José Martí was born in Havana, Cuba on January 28, 1853. His friends called him Pepe. His mother and father were born in Spain, and his father was a sergeant in the Spanish Army in Cuba. When he was 13, Martí entered St. Paul's School in Havana and was an excellent student. Rafael Mendive, a poet and journalist, was the director of the school and his teacher. Mendive was like a father to Martí and taught him to love literature, to write, and to dream of an independent Cuba.

When Martí was only 16, he was arrested with his best friend, Fermín Valdés, for writing a letter that criticized a classmate for joining the Spanish Army. Martí was accused of treason and was sentenced to six years of hard labor at the Presidio, a horrible prison. He spent six months in that hell before he was sent to another prison and then into exile in Spain.

He loved Spain and its museums, theaters, and universities, but he continued to speak out against the Spanish rule in Cuba. He studied in Madrid and Zaragoza and, in 1874, he received a law degree and a degree in literature from the University of Zaragoza. After he finished his studies, he went to live with his family in Mexico City.

In Mexico, Martí met and fell in love with the beautiful Carmen Zayas, who was also from Cuba. They were married on December 20, 1877, in Mexico City. They went to live in Guatemala, where he was a professor of history and literature at the university. In February 1878, the Ten Years' War between Spain and Cuba ended, and Martí and his wife returned to Cuba, where their son José was born on November 22, 1878. His birth was a great joy, but their marriage wasn't a happy one because Carmen didn't share or understand her husband's political activities and dedication to the liberation of Cuba.

Soon after Martí's return to Cuba, he was forced into exile again. He went to Spain and then to France and, in January 1880, to New York City, where he lived for 15 years. He was one of Latin America's best writers. He wrote poetry, essays, and newspaper and magazine articles. He was also a teacher and a popular speaker.

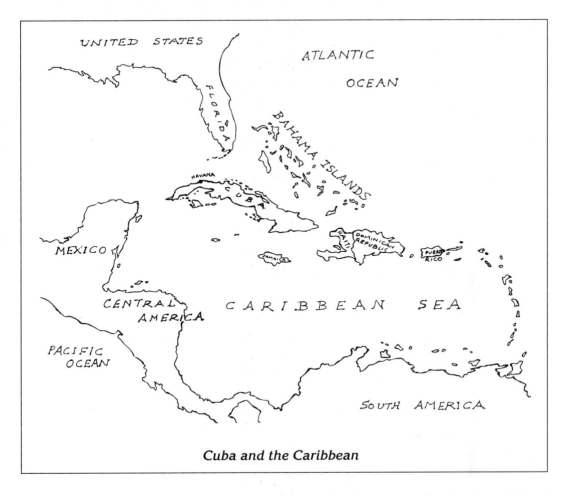

Cuba and the Caribbean

But, above all, Martí was the leader of the struggle for Cuban independence. He spent a lot of time planning, organizing, and collecting funds for the invasion of Cuba. He spoke at meetings in New York City and in Tampa and Key West, Florida to unify and inspire the Cuban exiles. By 1895, the preparations for the invasion of Cuba were complete. Antonio Gomez, the military commander of the invasion, wanted Martí to stay in New York, but Martí insisted on going to Cuba to fight and, if necessary, to die to free Cuba. Martí was killed in a battle at Dos Ríos, Cuba, on May 19, 1895. Seven years later, Cuba became an independent country. Martí is known as the Apostle[1] of Cuban Independence.

[1] An **apostle** is a person with a special mission.

I. Comprehension

Answer these questions about the story. Use your own ideas to answer questions marked with a check ✔.

Paragraph 1

1. What was José Martí's father?
2. Name three things that Martí learned from his teacher Rafael Mendive.

Paragraph 2

3. Why were Martí and his friend arrested?
✔ 4. How do you think Martí's father felt about his political activities? And his mother? Explain your answers.

Paragraph 3

5. Did Martí like Spain? How did he show that he didn't like the Spanish rule in Cuba?
6. What did Martí study and receive degrees in at the University of Zaragoza?

Paragraph 4

7. What happened to Martí in Mexico City?
8. Why wasn't his marriage happy?

Paragraph 5

9. Martí is one of Latin America's best writers. What did he write?

Paragraph 6

10. What was Martí, above all?
11. How did he spend much of his time?
✔ 12. Why do you think the United States was a good place to plan and organize the invasion of Cuba?

II. Key Words

Before studying these words, reread the story and try to guess their meaning.

Nouns			Verbs	Irregular Past
sergeant	prison	article	arrest (+n.)	spoke - speak
poet	professor	funds	accuse	
journalist	dedication	invasion	sentence (+n.)	
classmate	liberation	preparation	organize	**Adjective**
treason	essay	apostle	unify	horrible
			inspire	
			insist	

III. Story Completion

Complete the story with these words.

funds	classmate	horrible	inspire	journalist
dedication	arrested	liberation	treason	essays

Martí's Dream, an Independent Cuba

José Martí was born in Havana, Cuba on January 28, 1853. Rafael Mendive, a poet and _____ , taught Martí to love literature, to write, and to dream of an independent Cuba.

When Martí was only 16, he was _____ for writing a letter that criticized a _____ for joining the Spanish Army. He was accused of _____ and sentenced to six years of hard labor in a _____ prison.

On December 20, 1877, he married Carmen Zayas, but their marriage wasn't happy. She didn't share or understand Martí's political activities and _____ to freeing Cuba.

Martí wrote poetry, _____ , and newspaper and magazine articles and was one of Latin America's best writers.

But, above all, Martí was the leader of the struggle for Cuban independence. He planned, organized, and collected _____ for the _____ of Cuba. He spoke at meetings in New York City and Florida to unify and _____ the Cuban exiles.

IV. Dialogs

Key Words

Nouns	Verbs		Adjective	Other
palm tree	bother (+n)	count on	Yankee	else (adv.)
imperialism	annex (+n.)	support (+n.)		so (adv.)
patience	favor (+n.)			

Cold Weather and Imperialism

José Martí lived in exile in New York City from 1880 to 1895. In this interview, Martí is talking about the United States to a reporter.

Complete the dialog with these words.

annex   miss   imperialism   favor   bothers

Reporter: What do you think of the United States?

Martí: I like some things, but not others.

Reporter: What do you mean?

Martí: I like the freedom here. It's what we want for Cuba.

Reporter: And what don't you like?

Martí: The cold weather. I _____ the sun and

palm trees of Cuba.

Reporter: What else _____ you?

Martí: Yankee _____.

Reporter: Are you afraid the United States will _____ Cuba?

Martí: Yes, and that would kill me.

Reporter: But won't the United States, the land of the free,

_____ a free Cuba?

Martí: I hope so, but I'm afraid it won't.

We All Love Cuba

Martí was careful to include black Cubans in his plans to invade Cuba. He wanted a revolution "with all, and for the good of all." He is talking to Rafael Serra, a black Cuban leader. It's 1894, and they're in New York City.

Complete the dialog with these words.

unite	supporting	patience	exiles	count on

Serra: Is Cuba ready to fight again?

Martí: Almost, but we need unity, money, and _____.

Serra: Do you think you can _____ all Cubans, rich and poor, black and white?

Martí: Why not? We all love Cuba, but I need your help.

Serra: You can _____ me, but I have a question.

Martí: What is it?

Serra: Where's the money coming from?

Martí: From the many Cubans who are poor and the few who are rich.

Serra: Where are you going now?

Martí: To Tampa, Florida and then to Key West.

Serra: Why?

Martí: To talk to the Cuban _____ who work in the cigar factories.

Serra: About what?

Martí: About _____ an invasion of Cuba.

V. Sharing Ideas

Discuss these questions in pairs or small groups.

1. Martí wouldn't limit his political activity to please his wife, and she wouldn't support his political activity to please him. Do you think he was right? Or do you think she was right? Or is it impossible to say? Explain your answer.

2. Why was a lot of money needed for the invasion of Cuba?

3. Do you think it was foolish for Martí to risk his life by going to fight in Cuba? Explain your answer.

4. Martí liked some things about the United States, but not others. What do you like about the United States?

5. What don't you like?

6. What do you miss from your country?

7. Reread the life of Simón Bolívar (pages 138–140) and compare the lives of Bolívar and Martí. How were they alike? How were they different?

8. What do you know about Cuba? Where is it located? What are its main cities? What is its capital? How large is it? What is its population? Describe its climate. Describe its economy. What kind of government does it have? Have the students work in small groups. Each group should give a brief report answering two or three of the questions. One group should include a map of Cuba.

VI. Books You May Enjoy

1. Gleiter, Jan, and Kathleen Thompson. *José Martí*. Raintree Hispanic Stories. Milwaukee, Wisconsin: Raintree Publishers, 1989. 32 pp. (Level 1)

*2. Bailey, Bernadine. *Famous Latin-American Liberators*. New York: Dodd, Mead & Company, 1960. 158 pp. (Level 3)

* Books with an asterisk are for teachers. They are too difficult for students using *Leaders of the Americas*.

7

Social Pioneers

18 Susan B. Anthony

Susan B. Anthony

Important Events

February 15, 1820	Anthony is born in Adams, Massachusetts
1846–1849	Is a teacher and principal in Canajoharie, New York
1851	Meets Elizabeth C. Stanton
January 8, 1868	Publishes the newspaper *The Revolution*
1869	Forms National Woman Suffrage (Voting) Association
November 28, 1872	Is arrested for voting in Rochester, New York
March 13, 1906	Dies in Rochester, New York

Preview

1. Susan B. Anthony dedicated herself to obtaining equal rights for women, especially the right to vote. Why was the right to vote the key to obtaining other rights for women?

2. Susan B. Anthony worked hard to abolish slavery and to obtain equal rights for African Americans. Why was it natural for a person fighting for women's rights also to fight for the rights of African Americans?

Susan B. Anthony
(1820–1906)

On November 28, 1872, Susan B. Anthony was arrested for voting in Rochester, New York in a national election. At her trial, the judge said it was illegal for a woman to vote and fined her $100. Anthony told the judge she would never pay the fine and she never did.

Susan B. Anthony was born in Adams, Massachusetts on February 15, 1820. Her father was a devout Quaker[1] and a successful businessman. Her mother always had too much to do. Besides cooking, cleaning, washing, ironing, sewing, and caring for her husband and six children, she housed and fed the young women who worked at her husband's cotton mill.

Susan's father was a firm believer in education for girls as well as boys. He even sent Susan to a Quaker school for girls in Philadelphia. But a year later, in 1838, she had to return home because her father's business failed. To help support the family, she turned to teaching, about the only profession open to women. Anthony was disappointed and angry when she discovered they were paying her much less than a male teacher. From 1846 to 1849, she taught and was principal of a school in Canajoharie, New York, but she wanted to do more than teach.

Anthony became very active in the temperance movement, whose aim was to control the sale and use of alcohol. In 1851, she met Elizabeth Stanton, a leader in the fight to grant women the right to vote. They became the closest of friends, although they were very different. Stanton was short, heavy, married, and the mother of six. Anthony was tall, thin, and single. Stanton was a great writer, and Anthony was a great organizer. Over the years they worked together, devoting their time, energy, and talent to three causes: temperance, the abolition of slavery, and, above all, equal rights for women.

Anthony and Stanton hated slavery and worked hard with other abolitionist leaders to end it. However, after the Civil War they were disappointed when many abolitionists fought to obtain for black men, but not for women, the right to vote.

So Anthony and Stanton turned their attention more and more to one thing, obtaining equal rights for women, especially the right to vote. But

Susan B. Anthony Speaking at a Meeting

it was tough. The problem was that women needed political power to get the right to vote, but they had little political power because they couldn't vote.

Anthony traveled from state to state giving speeches, collecting petitions, and organizing groups. She addressed the lawmakers in Albany, the capital of New York, and in Washington, D.C. But many people hated Anthony and her message. They insulted her, threw eggs at her, and interrupted her speeches, but they never stopped her. She kept fighting for the right to vote until she died in 1906 at the age of 86. In 1920, 100 years after her birth, the Nineteenth Amendment to the Constitution finally gave women the right to vote.

---

1 The **Quakers**, or Society of Friends, are a group of Christians known for their opposition to war. They were also strongly opposed to slavery and did much to abolish it.

I. Comprehension

Answer these questions about the story. Use your own ideas to answer the questions marked with a check ✔.

Paragraph 1

1. Why was Susan B. Anthony arrested?
2. What did she tell the judge?

Paragraph 2

3. What was Anthony's father?
4. Besides taking care of her own family, who did her mother house and feed?

Paragraph 3

5. Why did Anthony have to return home?
✔ 6. Why do you think they paid female teachers less than males?

Paragraph 4

7. How were Stanton and Anthony different?
8. To what did they devote their time, energy, and talent?
✔ 9. Anthony was single. What advantages did that give her in working for her causes?

Paragraph 5

10. Why were Anthony and Stanton disappointed with many abolitionists?

Paragraph 6

11. Why was it tough for women to get the right to vote?

Paragraph 7

12. How did some people try to stop Anthony?

II. Key Words

Before studying these words, reread the story and try to guess their meaning.

Nouns		Verbs	Irregular Pasts	Adjectives
trial	aim (+v.)	fine (+n.)	fed - feed	illegal
judge (+v.)	organizer	iron (+n.)	threw - throw	devout
fine (+v.)	talent	fail	kept - keep	firm
cotton	abolition	support (+n.)		disappointed
mill	abolitionist	grant (+n.)		tough
profession	petition (+v.)	devote		
temperance	message	address		**Other**
movement		interrupt		as well as
				(conj.)

III. Story Completion

Complete the story with these words.

message	**failed**	**devout**	**abolition**	**interrupted**
fined	**tough**	**trial**	**as well as**	**aim**

Fighting for the Right to Vote

In 1872, Susan B. Anthony was arrested for voting. At her

_____ , the judge said it was illegal for a

woman to vote and _____ her $100.

Susan's father was a _____ Quaker and a

successful businessman. He believed in education for girls

_____ boys. He sent Susan to a school for girls

in Philadelphia, but she had to return home when her father's

business _____ .

Anthony became a teacher, but that wasn't enough for

her. She was active in the temperance movement, whose

_____ was to control the sale and use of alcohol. She also worked for the _____ of slavery and for equal rights for women.

Anthony fought hard to obtain for women the right to vote, but it was _____ because women had little political power since they couldn't vote.

Anthony gave speeches, collected petitions, and organized groups to get women the right to vote. But many people hated her _____. They insulted her, threw eggs at her, and _____ her speeches, but they never stopped her.

IV. Dialogs

Key Words

Nouns	Verbs		Adjective	Other
struggle (+v.)	agree	earn	fantastic	against (prep.)
property	bother	subscribe		

A Great Team

In 1851, Susan B. Anthony met Elizabeth Stanton. They became friends and worked together for the next 50 years. In those days, the money that a married woman earned belonged to her husband, and she couldn't own property.

Complete the dialog with these words.

earn   struggle   against   property   agree

Stanton: We can work together for women's rights and _____ drinking.

Anthony: Fantastic! I'm single, so I can travel and make speeches.

Stanton: And I can write them. I'm good at that.

Anthony: We're going to make a great team!

Stanton: What do you think women need most?

Anthony: The right to vote.

Stanton: I _____. But do you know what else bothers me?

Anthony: No. What?

Stanton: Every penny we _____ belongs to our husbands.

Anthony: True, and married women can't own _____.

Stanton: We have to change all that.

Anthony: I know, but it's going to be a long hard _____.

The Revolution

In 1868, Anthony started publishing a newspaper called *The Revolution*. She visited the White House to ask a busy President Andrew Johnson to subscribe to it.

Complete the dialog with these words.

right	support	subscribe	sign	already

Johnson: What can I do for you, Miss Anthony?

Anthony: I want you to _____ to our new newspaper.

Johnson: What's it called?

Anthony: *The Revolution*.

Johnson: What's it all about?

Anthony: Women's rights, especially the right to vote.

Johnson: I see. Frankly, I _____ get too many newspapers.

Anthony: But you want the _____ of women, don't you?

Johnson: Of course I do. You'll have to excuse me, Miss Anthony. I'm very busy.

Anthony: I won't say another word if you buy our newspaper.

Johnson: All right! All right! Where do I _____?

Anthony: _____ here! Thank you, Mr. President.

Johnson: Good day, Miss Anthony and good luck.

V. Sharing Ideas

Discuss these questions in pairs or small groups.

1. Why were cooking, cleaning, washing, ironing, and sewing more difficult in 1830 than today?

2. Do you think most husbands who don't help with the housework appreciate how much work goes into caring for a house and young children? Explain your answer.

3. In 1846, male teachers were paid more than females. Do female teachers today get the same pay as males?

4. Anthony and Stanton were active in the movement to limit and discourage the use of alcohol. Why was this movement so important to women, especially married women?

5. How old do you have to be to vote? What else is necessary?

6. Why is it important that all citizens vote? Do you vote? If not, is there a reason?

7. Today more and more women in the United States and other countries hold important political jobs. Name some women in the United States and in other countries who have important jobs in their governments.

8. Imagine that Susan Anthony is alive again. Write her a letter telling her what has happened since her death. Write especially about the rights of women.

VI. Books You May Enjoy

1. Grant, Matthew G. *Susan B. Anthony: Crusader for Women's Rights.* Gallery of Great Americans Series. Mankato, Minnesota: Creative Education, 1974. 31 pp. (Level 1)

2. Peterson, Helen Stone. *Susan B. Anthony: Pioneer in Woman's Rights.* Americans All Biographies. Champaign, Illinois: Garrard Publishing Company, 1971. 96 pp. (Level 2)

*3. Weisberg, Barbara. *Susan B. Anthony.* American Women of Achievement. New York: Chelsea House Publishers, 1988. 111 pp. (Level 3)

* Books with an asterisk are for teachers. They are too difficult for students using *Leaders of the Americas.*

19 Jane Addams

Jane Addams

Important Events

September 6, 1860	Jane Addams is born in Cedarville, Illinois
June 1881	Graduates from Rockford College in Illinois
1883–85 & 1887–88	Travels and studies in Europe
September 14, 1889	Opens Hull House in Chicago
1915–1929	Serves as president of Women's International League for Peace and Freedom
1931	Receives Nobel Peace Prize
May 21, 1935	Dies in Chicago at the age of 74

Preview

1. Jane Addams' family was rich, but she dedicated her life to the poor. Do you think most rich people help the poor in some way? Should they? How can they?

2. Many of those Jane Addams helped were Italian immigrants. She had been to Italy and was able to speak Italian. Do you think her knowledge of Italian and Italy was a big help in her work? Explain your answer.

Jane Addams
(1860–1935)

Jane Addams was born in the small town of Cedarville, Illinois on September 6, 1860. She was the youngest of eight children. Her father was a state Senator for many years and a prosperous businessman. Her mother died when she was two. Five years later, her father married Anna Haldeman, a widow. When Jane was 17, she entered Rockford College for Women.[1] She was a very good student, loved to read, and was a good debater. She was also the editor of the college newspaper and president of her senior class.

The summer after Addams graduated from Rockford, her father died of appendicitis. It was the saddest day of her life. Despite her sorrow, she entered the Women's Medical College in Philadelphia to study to be a doctor. She did well in her studies, but a bad back forced her to leave med school and have an operation. She was in bed for six months.

Addams spent the next two years studying and traveling in Europe with her stepmother and friends. She loved the great museums, paintings, and cathedrals of Europe, but she was shocked by the poverty she saw, especially in the slums of London. During a second trip to Europe, she decided to dedicate her life to helping the poor. She was 29.

Addams' plan was simple—to buy a house in a very poor neighborhood, live there, and help the poor. Her best friend, Ellen Starr, joined her, and they rented a large house in one of Chicago's poorest neighborhoods, the Nineteenth Ward. They named it Hull House after the man who first owned it.

The first thing Addams and Starr did was to open a day nursery to take care of the young children of working mothers. Before long, they had after-school activities for teenagers and, at night, English classes for adults. Most of the adults in the neighborhood were European immigrants and didn't know English.

Soon many volunteers came to live and work at Hull House. Addams and the volunteers helped people get jobs, started all kinds of clubs for children and adults, and built the first public playground in Chicago. By

Hull House

1909, 20 years after Hull House opened, it occupied an entire city block and had 13 buildings, including a gym, a theater, and an art gallery. Addams and Hull House had become famous, and many settlement houses similar to Hull House opened in other cities.

Addams, however, didn't limit her interests and activities to Hull House. During and after World War I, she worked hard for peace among nations. In 1915, she was elected president of the Women's International League for Peace and Freedom. Many criticized her for being a pacifist. Some even said that she was un-American, but that didn't make her change her mind. She felt strongly that nations should solve their problems not by war, but by talking and compromising. In 1931, Jane Addams received the Nobel Peace Prize for her work in promoting peace and cooperation among nations. She died in Chicago in 1935 at the age of 74.

[1] When Jane Addams attended Rockford, its name was Rockford Seminary. The name was changed to Rockford College the year after she graduated.

I. Comprehension

Answer these questions about the story. Use your own ideas to answer the questions marked with a check ✔.

Paragraph 1

    1. What was Jane Addams' father?

    2. Jane Addams was a leader. How did she show that in college?

Paragraph 2

    3. What did Addams do after her father's death?

    4. Why did she leave med school?

Paragraph 3

    5. What in Europe shocked Addams?

    6. What did she decide to do during her second trip there?

Paragraph 4

    7. What was Addams' plan?

✔ 8. Why do you think it was important for Addams to have a friend like Ellen Starr to share her work?

Paragraph 5

✔ 9. What do you think was the first reaction of the people of the neighborhood to Addams and Starr?

    10. What was the first thing Addams and Starr did?

Paragraph 6

    11. Name three things Addams and the volunteers did for the people.

Paragraph 7

    12. Why did people criticize Addams and even call her un-American?

II. Key Words

Before studying these words, reread the story and try to guess their meaning.

Nouns			Verbs	Adjectives
senator	operation	immigrant	shock (+n.)	prosperous
widow	stepmother	playground	dedicate	senior
debater	cathedral	gallery	occupy	saddest
editor	poverty	settlement house	limit (+n.)	simple
appendicitis	slum	pacifist	solve	entire
med school	nursery	prize	compromise (+n.)	
			promote	**Other**
				before long
				(idiom)

III. Story Completion

Complete the story with these words.

nursery	operation	prosperous	solve	settlement house
editor	entire	before long	poverty	compromising

Helping the Poor

Jane Addams was born in Illinois in 1860. Her father was a state Senator and a _____ businessman. Her mother died when she was two.

When Jane was 17, she entered Rockford College. She was a good student and the _____ of the college newspaper. Her father died the summer after her graduation from college. Despite her sorrow, she entered med school, but a bad back forced her to leave and have an _____.

Addams traveled in Europe and was shocked by the _____ she saw there. She decided to dedicate her life to helping the poor.

Addams rented a house in a poor Chicago neighborhood and, with Ellen Starr, opened a day _____ to take care of the children of working mothers. _____ , they had activities for teenagers and English classes for adults.

Twenty years later, Addams' _____ occupied an _____ city block and had 13 buildings.

Addams also worked hard for world peace. She believed that nations should _____ their problems not by war, but by talking and _____.

IV. Dialogs

Key Words

Verbs	Adjectives		Other
apply	bright	fantastic	close (to) (adv., adj.)
share (+n.)	far (+adv.)		yet (adv., conj.)

I Love to Study and Learn

Jane Addams wanted to go to Smith College in Massachusetts, but her father wanted her to stay close to home and go to Rockford College in Illinois.

Complete the dialog with these words.

still   bright   apply   especially   far

Jane: Dad, I want to go to college.

Father: Good. I knew you would. You're a _____ girl.

Jane: I want to go to Smith College in Massachusetts.

Father: That's too _____. I want you close to home.

Jane: Can't I even _____ to Smith?

Father: You can, but I _____ think you should go to Rockford.

Jane: Okay, I'll apply and we can decide later.

Father: That's fine. And what do you want to be?

Jane: A doctor. I want to help others, _____ the poor.

Father: Wonderful! But you'll have to study hard.

Jane: That's no problem. I love to study and learn new things.

What Do You Want to Do?

Jane Addams and her very close friend, Ellen Starr, were traveling in Spain when Jane decided to dedicate her life to helping the poor.

Complete the dialog with these words.

share   fantastic   laugh   yet   neighborhood

Jane: I'm tired of traveling around Europe.

Ellen: I understand, but what do you want to do?

Jane: Don't _____ when I tell you.

Ellen: I won't. I'm your best friend.

Jane: I'm going to buy a large house in a poor _____.

Ellen: What for?

Jane: To live there and _____ with the poor.

Ellen: What exactly are you going to do for them?

Jane: I don't know _____. I have to see what the people need.

Ellen: Do you know something?

Jane: Tell me.

Ellen: I like your idea. I want to join you.

Jane: That's _____! I'm so happy.

V. Sharing Ideas

Discuss these questions in pairs or small groups.

1. Jane Addams was the editor of her college newspaper. What does the editor of a newspaper do?

2. Do you like to travel and see new places? What are the advantages of travel? What's the big problem with it?

3. Jane Addams didn't go to the Nineteenth Ward with any plans except to find out what the people needed. Why was this good?

4. Addams started her work by opening a nursery for the children of working mothers. Why do you think a nursery was so important to the families in the neighborhood?

5. She also started English classes at night for adults from other countries. Why was it important that they learn English?

6. Jane Addams was one of the first social workers. What does a social worker do?

7. What qualities did she have that made her an excellent social worker?

8. Jane Addams was a pacifist. She was against all wars. Are you a pacifist? If so, explain why. Or do you think that some wars are necessary? If so, explain why.

VI. Books You May Enjoy

1. Peterson, Helen Stone. *Jane Addams: Pioneer of Hull House.* Discovery Book. Champaign, Illinois: Garrard Publishing Company, 1965. 80 pp. (Level 1)

2. Keller, Gail Faithfull. *Jane Addams.* New York: Thomas Y. Crowell Co., 1971. 41 pp. (Level 1)

3. Mooney, Elizabeth Comstock. *Jane Addams.* Chicago: Follett Publishing Company, 1968. 156 pages. (Level 2)

8

Great Inventors

20 Thomas Alva Edison

Thomas A. Edison

Important Events

February 11, 1847	Thomas Edison is born in Milan, Ohio
December 25, 1871	Marries Mary Stilwell in Newark, New Jersey
1876	Builds labs and buys house in Menlo Park, New Jersey
1877	Improves the telephone and invents the phonograph
1879	Invents the electric light
1886	Marries Mina Miller and moves to West Orange, New Jersey
October 18, 1931	Dies at his West Orange home at the age of 84

Preview

1. Thomas Edison, the great inventor, never completed the first grade, but his mother taught him at home, and he educated himself by reading. Why is reading so important to a good education?

2. Edison didn't work alone. He hired many assistants and worked in a lab with them. Why was this smart?

Thomas Alva Edison
(1847–1931)

Thomas Alva Edison was a famous inventor with over 1,000 patents, but he went to school for only three months. He didn't get along with his first grade teacher, so his mother took him out of school and taught him at home. He was a very curious child and asked a million questions. He also loved to read and to experiment. Edison was born in Milan, Ohio on February 11, 1847.

Edison's family moved to Port Huron, Michigan when he was seven. He built a chemistry lab in his basement and labeled all his chemical bottles "poison," so no one else would touch them. When Edison was 12, he got a job selling newspapers, candy, and sandwiches on the train that went from Port Huron to Detroit. He gave some of the money he earned to his mother and spent the rest on chemicals. Then he moved his lab from his basement to the baggage car of the train so he could experiment in his spare time.

Edison Experimenting with Chemicals

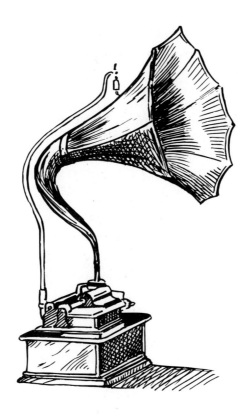

Edison's Phonograph

One day, Edison was in the telegraph office of a Mr. MacKensie. MacKensie's little boy was playing on the railroad track. Suddenly Edison saw a freight car heading for him. Edison ran, grabbed the little boy, and pushed him off the track just in time. Mr. MacKensie was extremely grateful. As a reward, he taught Edison how to operate a telegraph. After he learned, Edison got a job as a telegraph operator.

In 1869, Edison moved to New York City. There he greatly improved the stock ticker, a special telegraph that prints stock prices.[1] He was given $40,000 for the stock ticker, much more than he expected. Edison used the money to open his first lab and shop in Newark, New Jersey.

While in Newark, he fell in love with Mary Stilwell, and they got married on Christmas Day, 1871. Edison and his wife had three children. He loved his wife and children, but he didn't spend a lot of time with them. He often worked 20 hours a day in his lab and slept there. He was a workaholic.

In 1876, Edison moved to Menlo Park, New Jersey, where he bought a farmhouse and built a bigger lab. There he improved the telephone, which had been invented by Alexander Graham Bell. In 1877, Edison invented the phonograph, a talking machine. This was his favorite and most original invention. Then came his greatest invention, the electric light. It took 14 months, but Edison finally produced an electric light that was safe, bright, and cheap. People started calling him "The Wizard of Menlo Park."[2]

In 1884, Edison's wife died at the age of 29. He was terribly sad and lonely. Two years later, he married Mina Miller and moved to West Orange, New Jersey, where he bought a large home and built much bigger labs. It was there that he invented the motion picture camera and the storage battery. Edison died in his home at West Orange on October 18, 1931 at the age of 84. He was the greatest inventor in the history of the United States.

[1] **Stock** is the ownership of a company. It is divided into shares and sold. The price of stock goes up and down.

[2] A **wizard** is a person who is so good at doing something that he or she seems to have magical power. "Roger is a computer *wizard*. He knows more about computers than anyone in the college."

I. Comprehension

Answer these questions about the story. Use your own ideas to answer the questions marked with a check ✔.

Paragraph 1

1. Why did Edison's mother take him out of school?
2. Name two things Edison loved to do.

Paragraph 2

3. What was Edison's first job?
4. What did he do with the money he earned?

Paragraph 3

5. How did Edison save Mr. MacKensie's son from being hit by a freight car?
6. How did Mr. MacKensie reward him?

Paragraph 4

7. What did Edison do with the money he earned for the stock ticker?

Paragraph 5

8. Why didn't he spend more time with his wife and children?
✔ 9. Do you think he had many friends? Explain your answer.

Paragraph 6

10. What was Edison's favorite invention? And his greatest one?

Paragraph 7

✔ 11. After the death of his first wife, Edison didn't spend much time in Menlo Park. Why not?

12. What did he invent in West Orange, New Jersey?

II. Key Words

Before studying these words, reread the story and try to guess their meaning.

Nouns		Verbs	Adjectives
basement	railroad track	get along with	curious
chemical (+adj.)	freight	experiment (+n.)	chemical (+n.)
chemistry	stock ticker	label (+n.)	spare (+v.)
lab = laboratory	workaholic	grab	original
poison (+v.)	phonograph		bright
baggage	wizard	**Irregular Past**	
telegraph (+v.)	storage battery	slept - sleep	**Other**
			extremely (adv.)
			while (conj., n.)
			terribly (adv.)

III. Story Completion

Complete the story with these words.

original	extremely	chemicals	grabbed	while
experiment	baggage	bright	telegraph	spare

The Wizard of Menlo Park

Thomas Edison, the great inventor, went to school for only three months, but he was a very curious child, and he loved to read and to _____.

At 12, Edison got a job selling newspapers on a train. He gave some of the money he earned to his mother and spent the rest on _____. He moved the lab he had in his basement to the _____ car of the train so he could experiment in his _____ time.

One day, Edison saw a freight car heading for Mr. MacKensie's boy, who was playing on the railroad track. He _____ the boy and pushed him off the track just in time. Mr. MacKensie was _____ grateful and taught Edison how to operate a _____.

Edison opened his first lab and shop in Newark, New Jersey. _____ there, he married Mary Stilwell on Christmas Day, 1871. They had three children.

In 1876, Edison moved to Menlo Park, New Jersey, where he invented the phonograph, his most _____ invention. It was also at Menlo Park that he produced an electric light that was safe, _____ , and cheap. That was his greatest invention, and people started calling him "The Wizard of Menlo Park."

IV. Dialogs

Key Words

Nouns			Verbs	Adjectives	Other
gaslight	combination	inspiration	succeed	cheaper	so far (idiom)
oil lamp	perspiration	nap (+v.)		due	until (conj., prep.)
success					

Night into Day

Edison enjoyed talking to reporters. It's October 1878, and he's talking to a reporter about his work on the electric light.

Complete the dialog with these words.

cheaper	succeed	so far	positive	gaslights

Reporter: What is your greatest invention _____?

Edison: The phonograph, the machine that talks.

Reporter: Why?

Edison: For one thing, it's my most original invention.

Reporter: And what are you working on now?

Edison: An electric light.

Reporter: But we have _____ and oil lamps. Why do we need an electric light?

Edison: It'll be much brighter. It'll turn night into day.

Reporter: Will it be safe?

Edison: Very. It'll be safer, cleaner, and _____ than gaslight.

Reporter: How long will it take to invent?

Edison: Maybe six weeks. Maybe six months or more. I don't know.

Reporter: Are you sure it can be done?

Edison: I'm _____. And I won't stop until I

_____.

Hard Work and Good Ideas

A reporter is asking Edison why he's so successful. He says it's due mostly to hard work, to perspiration.

Complete the dialog with these words.

due	combination	naps	success	inspiration

Reporter: What's the secret of your _____?

Edison: It's a _____ of things.

Reporter: Of what?

Edison: Hard work and good ideas, perspiration and

_____.

Reporter: How much is _____ to hard work?

Edison: Ninety-nine percent.

Reporter: Are you saying only one percent is due to good ideas?

Edison: That's right.

Reporter: And is true that you sleep only four hours a night?

Edison: Yes it is, but I also take short _____.

V. Sharing Ideas

Discuss these questions in pairs or small groups.

1. Edison always asked a lot of questions. Do you think this helped him be an inventor? Explain your answer.
2. Edison loved to experiment, to try new ways of doing things. Do you?
3. Edison felt his success was due more to his hard work than to his ideas. What do you think is more important to success—hard work or good ideas?
4. Edison was famous for his ability to do without much sleep. How many hours of sleep do you think you need? How many do you usually get?
5. Edison was also famous for his naps. Do you ever take naps? Often?

6. Do you think Edison should have spent more time with his wife and children? Explain your answer.

7. We don't use phonographs today. What do we use instead?

8. Reread the life of Benjamin Franklin (pages 32–34). Compare the lives of Edison and Franklin. How were they alike? How were they different?

VI. Books You May Enjoy

1. Sabin, Louis. *Thomas Alva Edison: Young Inventor*. Mahwah, New Jersey: Troll Associates, 1983. 48 pp. (Level 1)

2. Martin, Patricia Miles. *Thomas Alva Edison*. See & Read–Beginning to Read Biographies. New York: G.P. Putnam's Sons, 1971. 63 pp. (Level 1)

3. Kaufman, Mervyn D. *Thomas Alva Edison: Miracle Worker*. A Discovery Book. Champaign, Illinois: Garrard Publishing Company, 1962. 80 pp. (Level 1)

4. Davidson, Margaret. *The Story of Thomas Alva Edison: The Wizard of Menlo Park*. Scholastic Biography. New York: Scholastic, Inc., 1990. 61 pp. (Level 2)

5. Weinberg, Michael. *What Was It Like? Thomas Edison*. What Was It Like? Series. Stamford, Connecticut: Longmeadow Press, 1988. 48 pp. (Level 2)

21 Wilbur & Orville Wright

The Wright Brothers Repairing Bicycles

Important Events

April 16, 1867	Wilbur Wright is born near Milville, Indiana
August 19, 1871	Orville Wright is born in Dayton, Ohio
1892	Wright brothers open a bicycle shop in Dayton
1900, 1901, 1902	They test gliders at Kitty Hawk, North Carolina
December 17, 1903	They fly a power-driven airplane at Kitty Hawk
Aug. 1908 – Jan. 1909	Wilbur demonstrates Wright plane in France
September 1908	Orville demonstrates Wright plane at Fort Myer, Virginia
May 13, 1917	Wilbur dies in Dayton at the age of 45
January 30, 1948	Orville dies in Dayton at the age of 76

Preview

1. On December 17, 1903, at Kitty Hawk, North Carolina, Orville Wright became the first person to fly a plane. He flew 120 feet, and his flight lasted 12 seconds. When was the last time you flew? Where did you fly from? And to? About how many miles did you fly? How long did your flight last?

2. Do you think the first flights made by Wilbur and Orville Wright were very dangerous? Explain your answer. When you fly, how much do you worry about a crash? A lot? A little? Not at all?

The Wright Brothers

Wilbur Wright was born on a farm near Milville, Indiana on April 16, 1867. His younger brother, Orville, was born four years later in Dayton, Ohio on August 17, 1871. The Wright brothers were like twins. They had the same interests; they played, worked, and planned together. But they were also different. Wilbur worked slowly, was quiet, and very serious. Orville worked fast and liked to talk and to joke.

Wilbur and Orville were both good students, especially in math, but they were best at fixing and making things. They made the finest kites in Dayton, and that was the beginning of their interest in flying.

The First Airplane Flight at Kitty Hawk

Orville built a printing press with Wilbur's help, and they published their own newspaper, the *West Side News*. But they couldn't compete with the other Dayton newspapers. Then they started to repair bicycles. Soon they were making and selling their own bikes at the Wright Cycle Company. But more and more, Wilbur and Orville were talking, reading, and dreaming about one thing—flying. They spent hours observing birds in flight and reading everything they could find about flying.

Their next step was to build and experiment with gliders, aircraft that fly on wind currents. They built a glider in the back of their bicycle shop and, in the summer of 1900, shipped it to the small fishing village of Kitty Hawk, North Carolina to test. They chose Kitty Hawk because it had steady winds, no trees, and miles of soft sand to land on. For three summers, they tested and improved their gliders.

Then in Dayton, in 1903, the Wright brothers built an airplane with a motor and two propellers. In the fall, they returned to Kitty Hawk. And on December 17, 1903, Orville became the first person in history to fly an airplane. They called the plane Flyer 1.[1] Orville flew it for 12 seconds and went 120 feet. They made three more flights that day. On the last one, Wilbur flew for 59 seconds and went 852 feet. Five people watched their flights, but only a few newspapers reported them.

In the next two years, the Wright brothers built and flew new planes and greatly improved them. They tested them in a cow pasture near Dayton. But many people didn't believe these flights ever took place, and it wasn't until 1908 that they showed the world they could fly. In May of that year, Wilbur sailed to France to demonstrate their new Type A Flyer. Between August 1908 and January 1909, he flew over 100 flights near Le Mans, France. The flights were a great success, and thousands of people came from all over Europe to see them. In September of 1908, Orville went to Fort Myer, Virginia, where he successfully demonstrated the Type A Flyer to the U.S. Army. The Wright brothers had finally proved their claims, and the Age of Flight had begun.

Wilbur Wright died in 1912 of typhoid fever when he was only 45, but Orville lived a long life. He died in 1948 of a heart attack at the age of 77.

[1] **Flyer 1** is on display at the Smithsonian National Air and Space Museum in Washington, D.C.

I. Comprehension

Answer these questions about the story. Use your own ideas to answer the questions marked with a check ✔.

Paragraph 1

1. Which of the Wright brothers was older? How much older?
2. How were Wilbur and Orville Wright different?

Paragraph 2

3. What did the Wright brothers do best?
4. What was the beginning of their interest in flying?

Paragraph 3

5. What did they make and sell at their company?
6. What did they talk, read, and dream about?

Paragraph 4

✔ 7. Do you think the Wright brothers were brave? Explain your answer.
8. Why did they go to Kitty Hawk, North Carolina to test their glider?

Paragraph 5

9. What did their airplane have that their gliders didn't?
10. How long did Orville's first flight on December 17, 1903 last? How far did he fly?

Paragraph 6

11. Where did Wilbur go to fly in 1908? How many flights did he make there?
✔ 12. Why do you think the U.S. Army wanted to have airplanes?

II. Key Words

Before studying these words, reread the story and try to guess their meaning.

Nouns		Verbs	Irregular Past	Adjective
twin	currents	compete	flew - fly	steady
printing press	sand	observe		
flight	propeller	land (+n.)		**Other**
glider	pasture	demonstrate		successfully (adv.)
aircraft	claim (+v.)			
step (+v.)	display (+v.)			
	typhoid fever			

III. Story Completion

Complete the story with these words.

pasture	compete	sand	joke	steady
flights	demonstrated	twins	flew	claims

Flyer 1

Wilbur and Orville Wright were like _____,
but they were also very different. Wilbur was a slow worker, quiet,
and serious. Orville was a fast worker and liked to talk and
_____.

The Wright brothers published their own newspaper for a while,
but they couldn't _____ with the other
Dayton newspapers. So they opened a bicycle shop.

Wilbur and Orville Wright built gliders in Dayton and tested
them at Kitty Hawk, North Carolina because it had _____
winds, no trees, and miles of soft _____ to
land on.

At Kitty Hawk, North Carolina, on December 17, 1903, the
Wright brothers made four historic _____ in
Flyer 1. Orville _____ for 12 seconds and went
120 feet. Later that day, Wilbur went 852 feet in 59 seconds.

In the next two years, the Wright brothers tested new and
better planes in a cow _____ near Dayton, but
many didn't believe these flights ever took place.

In 1908, the Wright brothers finally proved their _____.
Wilbur went to France and _____ a Type A Flyer to thousands of Europeans, and Orville successfully flew the same plane for the army at Fort Myer, Virginia.

IV. Dialogs

Key Words

Nouns		Irregular Past	Adjectives	Other
list (+v.)	reply (+v.)	heard - hear	tough	just (adv., adj.)
privacy	beach		terrific	

We're Going to Fly

Wilbur and Orville Wright wanted to be the first to fly. They started by watching birds, reading, and asking Professor Langley of the Smithsonian Institute in Washington for help.

Complete the dialog with these words.

list	gliders	observing	tough	enough

Orville: Someday, Wilbur, we're going to fly.

Wilbur: That's our dream, but it won't be easy.

Orville: I know it's going to be _____, but we can do it.

Wilbur: We should start by _____ how birds fly.

Orville: And by reading all we can about flying.

Wilbur: That's right. I'll check the Dayton Library.

Orville: What do you think of writing Professor Langley?

Wilbur: Great! I'll write and ask for a _____ of books on flying.

Orville: But reading isn't _____. We have to do our own testing.

Wilbur: Of course. We'll begin by testing _____.

Orville: Perfect. We can build one in our bike shop.

Wilbur: And test it in the late summer and fall.

Kitty Hawk, North Carolina

The Wright brothers need a place with steady winds and no trees to test their gliders. They turn to the Weather Bureau in Washington, D.C., for help.

Complete the dialog with these words.

reporters   just   beach   privacy   reply

Wilbur: Where are we going to test our glider?

Orville: We need a place with steady winds.

Wilbur: And no trees.

Orville: And _____.

Wilbur: Right. We don't want a lot of _____ around.

Orville: How can we find a place like that?

Wilbur: I'll write to the Weather Bureau in Washington, D.C.

Orville: Good idea! Why didn't I think of that?

[ten days later]

Wilbur: I have a _____ from the Weather Bureau.

Orville: What do they say?

Wilbur: Kitty Hawk is the best place.

Orville: Kitty Hawk? I never heard of it. Where's Kitty Hawk?

Wilbur: _____ off the coast of North Carolina. It's on an island.

Orville: Is it windy?

Wilbur: Always, and it has a large sandy _____.

Orville: That's terrific.

V. Sharing Ideas

Discuss these questions in pairs or small groups.

1. Orville Wright worked fast, but Wilbur worked slowly and carefully. Are you a fast worker like Orville, or are you a slow and careful one like Wilbur?

2. Are you good at fixing and making things?

3. What do you think the Wright brothers learned from flying kites that helped them build and fly gliders and airplanes?

4. Benjamin Franklin was also famous for an experiment with a kite. Do you remember what Franklin proved with the help of a kite?

5. Do you have a bicycle? Do you ride it much?

6. Wilbur and Orville Wright wanted to test their gliders and airplane where there were no trees. Why?

7. On December 13, 1903, the Wright brothers made history with their flights at Kitty Hawk. The next day only a few newspapers reported these flights. Why?

8. Reread the the life of Thomas Edison (pages 182–184). Compare the Wright brothers and Edison. How were they similar? How were they different?

VI. Books You May Enjoy

1. Sabin, Louis. *Wilbur and Orville Wright: The Flight to Adventure.* Mahwah, New Jersey: Troll Associates, 1983. 48 pp. (Level 1)

2. Hook, Jason. *The Wright Brothers.* Great Lives Series. New York: The Bookwright Press, 1989. 32 pp. (Level 1)

3. Tomes, Richard. *The Wright Brothers.* Lifetimes Biographical Series. New York: Franklin Watts, 1990. 32 pp. (Level 1)

4. Freedman, Russell. *The Wright Brothers: How They Invented the Plane.* New York: Holiday House, 1991. 128 pp. (Level 2)

*5. Welch, Becky. *The Wright Brothers: Conquering the Sky.* Great Lives Series. New York: Fawcett, Columbine, 1992. 120 pp. (Level 3)

* Books with an asterisk are for teachers. They are too difficult for students using *Leaders of the Americas.*

Word List

The words used to fill in the blanks in the story-completion exercises and the dialogs are listed below.

A

abolish 92
abolition 167
above all 141
accomplish 47
across 142
admire 130
affairs 45
against 103, 168
agree 7, 168
agreement 15
aim 167
allow 94
already 169
although 24, 141
among 75
annex 158
apply 103, 176
appoint 57, 103
appointment 8
appreciate 112
approach 131
argue 110
arrest 157
as well as 167
athletic 45
attach 37
attack 142
attract 37

B

badly 46
baggage 185
bandage 110
bargain 67
beach 197
beat 151
before long 175
belong 111
born 8

bother 158
brave 7, 142
bravery 112
brick 130
bright 58, 176, 185
brilliant 46
bullet 110
business 69

C

camp 25
candle 35
cane 123
captain 8
chains 121
challenge 76
cheaper 187
chemicals 185
chief 15
chose 15, 75
citizen 67
claim 195
classmate 157
clearer 36
clever 123
climate 76
colony 26
collect 36
combination 26, 188
commander 104
compete 195
complain 67
compromise 175
concern 94
consider 47, 105
construct 130
contend 75
convention 45
convert 26
cooperate 131
count on 159

courage 15, 110
crazy 9
create 68
criticize 67
cross 9, 46

D

dangerous 37
dawn 46
dead 85
debt 69
dedication 157
defense 17
delight 57
demonstrate 195
despite 149
destroy 141
detailed 75
devout 167
discourage 46, 141
disguise 123
double 67
draw 24
dream 7, 142
due 188
duty 103

E

eager 129
earn 168
editor 175
either 17
eliminate 149
enough 105, 150, 196
entire 175
equal 67
especially 176
essay 157
establish 110
even 35
evil 92

exaggerate 131
except 75
exile 149, 159
expand 129
expensive 8
experience 75
experiment 185
extremely 185

F

face 94
fail 167
fair 45
fairly 24
fantastic 177
far 7, 176
favor 158
federal 69
finally 7
finances 57
find 25, 76
fine (verb) 167
flee 141
flew 195
flight 195
fond 83
fool 122
foreign 149
forest 24
fought 45
found 24
frankly 105
freeze 122
friendship 17
funds 157

G

gaslight 187
get along 35
glider 196
goal 75
got 59
grab 185
graduate 58
grew up 103
guide 85

H

harm 112
harvest 15
have to 59
head (verb) 121, 151
healthy 84
hesitate 129
hide 121
highly 104
hire 16, 83
honor 130
horrible 157
hostility 77
humor 95
hunt 45, 77

I

imperialism 158
improve 24
in a row 92
in charge of 103
influence 47, 111
insist 131
inspiration 188
inspire 157
interests 67
interpreter 83
interrupt 167
invent 35
involve 112
issue 92
itself 111

J

join 84, 151
joke 195
journal 77
journalist 157
just 95, 197

K

kite 35

L

laugh 177
lawmaker 57
lead 104

led 24, 121
left 75
let 105
liberate 141
liberation 157
list 196
load 110
lobby 57
lodging 129
lonely 16, 121
look for 25
lost 92
luck 9
lucky 58

M

maid 121
main 67
major 141
manual 129
massive 149
matter 143, 150
mean 68, 104
meeting 47
message 167
miss 16, 158
mission 59, 75
moonlight 7
mourn 67

N

nap 188
near (verb) 151
neighborhood 177
nursery 175

O

observe 76, 196
occupation 57
of course 150
operation 175
opinion 35
organize 35
original 185

P

pasture 195
patience 159

200 Word List

permission 58, 110
persuade 7
plow 92
point 68
positive 187
pound 36
poverty 175
praise 103
pregnant 83
press 69
pressure 149
privacy 197
profitable 24
progress 129
property 121, 168
propose 150
prosperous 175
protect 26
protection 16
proud 85
prove 35
publish 35
puddle 77
purchase 67
pursuit 68

Q

queen 8
quickly 143
quit 141

R

raise 57
recognize 123
recommend 129
records 25
reduce 69
refuse 45
regret 103
remember 36
reply 197
report 122
reporter 197
represent 105
resign 104
respect 58
responsibility 149

restore 92
return 85
reunite 94
rewards 121
right 169
risk 83
root 75
round 9
route 76

S

sail 25
sand 195
satisfy 122
saying 36
self-help 130
sent 149
separate 15
settle 15
settlement house 175
share 57, 177
ship 9
shout 143
shovel 129
shy 110
sign (verb) 15, 169
sign (noun) 122
slave 83
smart 95
so 95
so far 77, 187
solve 175
spare 185
spent 24
spices 7
spread 92
spy 121
stay out 112
steady 195
steer 83
still 68, 143, 176
storm 15
stream 15
string 37
stronger 47
struggle 141, 168
subscribe 169

succeed 187
success 35, 188
successful 45
such a 85
sudden 83
suggest 17
supplies 7
support 59, 159, 169
supporter 57
surrender 103
surround 83
sword 143

T

taught 57
telegraph 185
theoretical 131
thrill 129
tough 84, 167, 196
trade 24
train 16
traitor 151
treason 157
treaty 17
trial 167
trouble (verb) 111
trust 123
turn back 7
turning point 103
twins 195
tyranny 141

U

understand 26
understanding 150
unite 142, 159
unload 129
upset 95

V

village 149
voice 110
volunteer 110

W

weak 45
while 185

whip 121
widow 37
wild 83
win 59
withdraw 149

wonder 45
wonderful 84
woods 92
worry 84
wounded 110

wrestler 92
wrong 94

Y

yet 177

Photograph and Illustration Credits

Page 3 – Bettmann

Page 5 – Adapted from Grosset, Joyce and Atwood, Elizabeth. *Great Explorers*. Grand Rapids, MI: Fideler Company/Gateway Press, 1961, p. 34

Page 19 – Culver Pictures, Inc.

Page 31 – Library of Congress

Page 41 – No credit

Page 52 – George M. Cushing Photography

Page 55 – Adapted from Harris & Gifford, Washington, D.C.

Page 65 – Colonial Studio

Page 71 – Adapted from Independence National Historical Park Collection.

Page 79 – John Morrell & Company

Page 89 – Library of Congress

Page 97 – Adapted from Association for the Studio of African American Life and History, Washington, D.C.

Page 99 – U.S. Signal Corps.

Page 117 – Bettmann

Page 125 – Bettmann

Page 137 – Philip D. Geudneau

Page 145 – No Credit

Page 153 – Culver Pictures, Inc.

Page 163 – Bettmann

Page 171 – Chicago Historical Society

Page 181 – AP/Wide World Photos

Page 183 – Adapted from North, Sterling. *Young Thomas Edison*. Boston: Houghton Mifflin Company, 1958, p. 161.

Page 191 – Smithsonian Institution